P · O · C · K · E · T · S

GEMSTONES

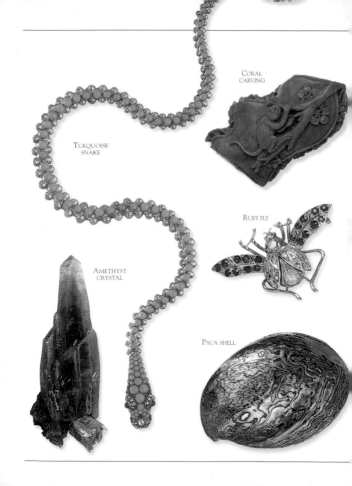

CORAL
CARVING

TURQUOISE
SNAKE

RUBY FLY

AMETHYST
CRYSTAL

PAUA SHELL

P · O · C · K · E · T · S

GEMSTONES

Written by
EMMA FOA

DIAMOND

EMERALD
LIZARD

ART DECO
CLIP

DK

DORLING KINDERSLEY
London • New York • Stuttgart • Moscow • Sydney

A DORLING KINDERSLEY BOOK

Project editor	Joanna Buck
Designer	Clair Watson
Senior editor	Alastair Dougall
Senior art editors	Carole Oliver
	Sarah Crouch
Picture research	Maureen Sheerin
Production	Kate Oliver
Editorial consultants	Sue Rigby
	Stephen Bradshaw

First published in Great Britain in 1997
by Dorling Kindersley Limited
9 Henrietta Street, Covent Garden, London WC2E 8PS

Copyright © 1997 Dorling Kindersley Ltd, London

Visit us on the World Wide Web at
http://www.dk.com

A CIP catalogue record for this book is available from
the British Library

ISBN 0 7513 5596 8

Colour reproduction by Colourscan, Singapore
Printed and bound in Italy by L.E.G.O.

CONTENTS

How to use this book

These pages show you how to use *Pockets: Gemstones*. The book is divided into five sections. These contain information about mineral, organic, and imitation gems, and an easy-to-use colour key. There is an introductory section at the front, and a reference section at the back, as well as a glossary and comprehensive index.

HEADING
The heading describes the overall subject of the page. This page is about emeralds. If a subject continues over several pages, the same heading applies.

CAPTIONS AND ANNOTATIONS
Each illustration has an explanatory caption. Some also have annotations, in *italics*, which point out the features of an illustration.

CORNER CODING
The corners of the main section pages are colour coded.

█ COLOUR KEY

█ MINERAL GEMSTONES

█ ORGANIC GEMSTONES

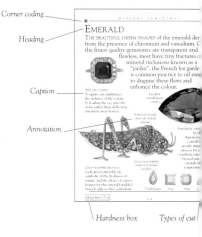

Corner coding

Heading

Caption

Annotation

EMERALD
THE BEAUTIFUL GREEN SHADES of the emerald deri from the presence of chromium and vanadium. C the finest quality gemstones are transparent and flawless, most have tiny fractures a mineral inclusions known as a "jardin", the French for garde is common practice to oil eme to disguise these flaws and enhance the colour.

Hardness box

Types of cut

HARDNESS SCALE
The hardness of each gem is indicated in a box on the bottom left-hand corner of the main gemstone pages. The numbers given are taken from Mohs' scale of hardness (see pages 24–5).

RUNNING HEADS
These remind you which
section you are in. The
top of the left-hand page
gives the section name,
and the top of the right-
hand page gives the
subject heading.

LABELS
For clarity, some pictures
have labels. These
may give extra
information about
the picture, or make
identification easier.

Label

MYTH AND MAGIC
The main gemstone
pages have boxes that
provide at-a-glance
information about the
myths and legends
surrounding each gem.

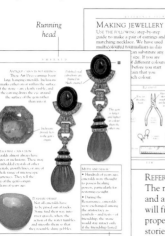

Running head

EMERALD

ANTIQUE COLOUR-IN EARRING
These Art Deco earrings from
large, hanging emeralds. Inclusions
marks either on or within the surface
of the stone – are clearly visible, and
the carving dents the eye around the
surface of the gem rather
than into it.

Polished oval
cabochons are
framed in
black enamel

*This gem
is lighter
in colour
than the
other two*

TALISMAN CABOCHON
Emeralds almost always have
naws or inclusions. These may be
embedded crystals of other
minerals, growth lines, or one of
a whole range of microscopic
occurrences. They tell the
story of the gem's origin –
millions of years ago.

Inclusions
provide keys
to the gem's
origin

POLISHED PEBBLE
Not all emeralds have
to be prised out of rocks.
Some find their way into
river gravels, where the
action of the water tumbles
and smooths them so that
they resemble shiny pebbles.

MYTH AND MAGIC
• Hundreds of years ago,
emeralds were thought
to possess healing
powers, particularly for
restoring eyesight.
• During the
Renaissance, emeralds
were exchanged among
the aristocracy as
symbols – and tokens – of
friendship; the stone
would stay intact only if
the friendship lasted.

Myth and magic box

MAKING JEWELLERY
USE THE FOLLOWING step-by-step
guide to make a pair of earrings and
matching necklace. We have used
multicoloured tourmalines in this
... can substitute other
... size. If you are
... different colours,
... before you start
... each colour.

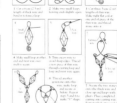

REFERENCE SECTION
The reference section pages are tinted yellow
and appear at the back of the book. Here you
will find a chart giving each gem's physical
properties, tips for looking after jewellery,
stories about famous gems, and a step-by-step
guide for making a necklace and earrings set.

GEMSTONE CUTS
Symbols appear on the bottom
of the left hand pages in the
main sections. These illustrate
the most popular cuts for each
gem (see page 29).

GLOSSARY AND INDEX
At the back of the book, there is a glossary
and index. By referring to the index,
information on particular topics can be
found quickly. The glossary defines the
technical terms used in the book.

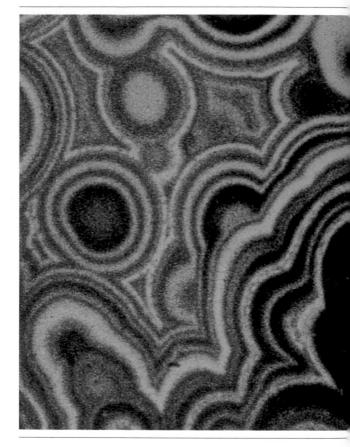

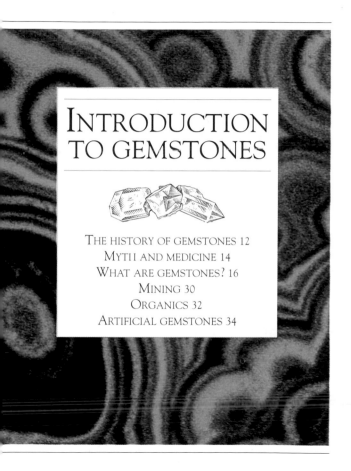

INTRODUCTION TO GEMSTONES

THE HISTORY OF GEMSTONES

THE STORY OF GEMSTONES is as old as the hills in which they formed, millions of years ago. Gleaning our knowledge from ancient burial sites, we know that gems were used for weapons as well as for adornment. "Jewels", ranging from humble seashells to rough emeralds, have been found in graves dating back 20,000 years.

NECKLACE FROM
THE COOK ISLANDS,
OCEANIA

Local stones

In the past, people worked mainly with local gemstones. Jade was carved in China 4,500 years ago; Egyptian and Sumerian craftsmen used lapis, carnelian, and turquoise; and the Romans carved agate. In the East, diamonds, rubies, and sapphires were popular.

Beetle,
symbol
of rebirth

NECKLACE
Shells have always been used for adornment. This necklace dates from about AD 990 and was worn by an island chief.

WINGED SCARAB
Egyptian craftsmen combined amber, lapis lazuli, carnelian, and turquoise in this scarab beetle good-luck charm. It was found in Tutankhamun's tomb and dates to 1360 BC.

Carved bands
of black and
white agate

LAPIS AND
CARNELIAN
NECKLACE

Cameo
of owner

ROMAN BROOCH
The original owner
of this beautiful
brooch must
have been a
wealthy man. Few
people could have afforded to
have their portrait carved in
agate and then set in gold filigree.

Amethyst bead

TIBETAN NOMAD
Today, jewellery is an
important part of many
peoples' national dress.
Large turquoise pebbles
form the basis of this
dramatic contemporary
necklace from Tibet.
Turquoise is a popular
feature of Tibetan
jewellery. It is
obtained locally
and is believed to
have talismanic
properties.

Etched
carnelian

BEADS FOR THE NEXT LIFE
In ancient times, it was
common practice for the
wealthy to be buried with
symbols of their status. This
lapis and carnelian necklace
was found in a Sumerian
grave in the 1st century BC.

MYTH AND MEDICINE

THE BEAUTY OF GEMS, their shimmering colours and perfect forms, led people to believe that they came from the heavens. Superstitions grew up around them, and different stones were deemed able to do everything from curing drunkenness to calming the roughest seas.

MAGIC LAPIS BRACELET
This Egyptian bracelet was buried alongside its owner. The eye was protective.

Healing powers

The alleged power of gemstones extended beyond the supernatural – gems were thought to have medicinal properties. Chinese and Ayurvedic medicines still involve gemstones, and healing with crystals is a growing art.

GROUND LAPIS LAZULI
Powdered lapis, taken in pill form, is a regular constituent of traditional Chinese medicine. In the past, gemstones were sometimes placed on an injured part of the body.

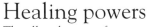

PEARL FACE CREAM
In China, powdered pearl is prescribed for skin complaints. Pearl cream is used for the face.

CRYSTAL BALL
For centuries, balls made out of polished rock crystal have been used to "see into the future".

Powdered lapis lazuli

14

LEOPARD-CLAW NECKLACE
Warriors used to believe that
they took on the powers of
the animals they killed. This
Nigerian necklace would thus
have been talismanic as well as
decorative – the hunter who
wore it would have thought
he was invincible.

Onyx
banding

Leopard's
claw

BUFFALO FETISH
North American
Indians once used stone
fetishes (magical
objects), such as this
onyx buffalo, to
attempt to influence
the forces of nature.

December –
turquoise

January –
garnet

February –
amethyst

November –
topaz

October –
opal

March –
aquamarine

BIRTHSTONES
Gems have been
associated with
different months of
the year since the
1st century AD. The
wearing of birthstones
was, and still is, deemed
lucky. It first became a
popular custom in the
18th century, in Poland.

September –
sapphire

Rock crystal engraved
with signs of the zodiac

April –
diamond

July –
ruby

June
pearl

August –
peridot

May –
emerald

WHAT ARE GEMSTONES?

TO BE CONSIDERED A GEM, a substance has to be
beautiful, usually in terms of its colour and the way
it reflects light. It also has to be rare and durable.
Gems are either minerals, which have a regular
internal structure and fixed chemical
composition, or organics, which
are produced by plants and animals.

Ruby crystal

MINERAL GEMS
The majority
of gems, like the
ruby shown here,
are minerals that
crystallize within
the Earth's crust.
Ruby forms at high
temperatures and pressures
and is brought to the Earth's
surface by rising magma or by
prolonged erosion.

NATURAL CRYSTAL
Ruby crystals form in igneous
and metamorphic rocks. They
are sometimes washed out of
these rocks into
river gravels.

CUT STONES
Rubies are
second only
to diamonds
in terms of
hardness. They
are prized for the richness of their
colour and their rarity. Rubies are
one of the most expensive gems.

CABOCHON CUT
Before deciding on a cut,
the gemstone cutter
will inspect
the crystal.
Cabochon cuts
reveal a star
effect when
certain markings
are present.

Star-effect ruby

SYNTHETIC GEMS

Synthetic gems are created in laboratories and have similar chemical properties to real gemstones. This synthetic ruby was manufactured by the Verneuil method (see page 34).

Crystals growing

Synthetic ruby

FLUX-MELT TECHNIQUE

French chemist Edmond Frémy discovered a method for growing ruby crystals by melting aluminium oxide and chromium in a crucible.

Ruby crystals in matrix

ORGANICS

Organic gems are produced by living organisms. This group includes jet, pearl, coral, amber, ivory, and shell. Organics are softer than mineral gems and usually opaque. They tend to be carved and polished rather than faceted (cut).

Oyster shell

Pearl bead

Round, faceted ruby

JEWELLERY

Gemstones are generally faceted and mounted so that light can shine through. This ruby and diamond cluster brooch dates from about 1915.

RUBY AND DIAMOND BROOCH

PEARL IN OYSTER SHELL

1 7

World map

Deposits of gemstones have been found in virtually every part of the world. They are dependent on particular geological conditions, which is why some stones are much rarer than others.

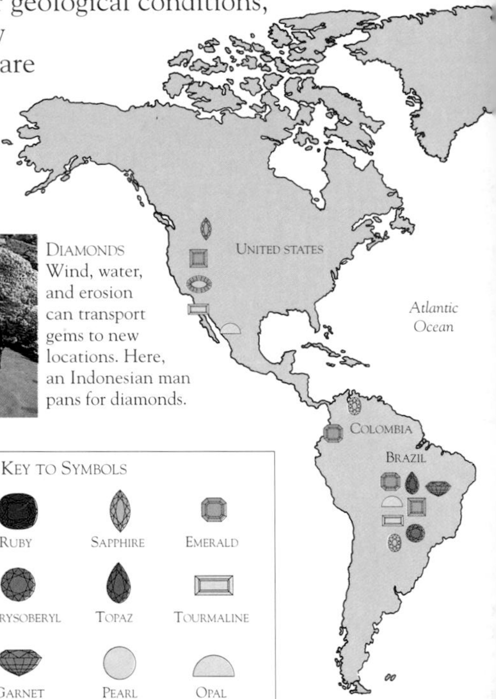

DIAMONDS
Wind, water, and erosion can transport gems to new locations. Here, an Indonesian man pans for diamonds.

UNITED STATES

Atlantic Ocean

COLOMBIA

BRAZIL

KEY TO SYMBOLS

DIAMOND	RUBY	SAPPHIRE	EMERALD
AQUAMARINE	CHRYSOBERYL	TOPAZ	TOURMALINE
PERIDOT	GARNET	PEARL	OPAL

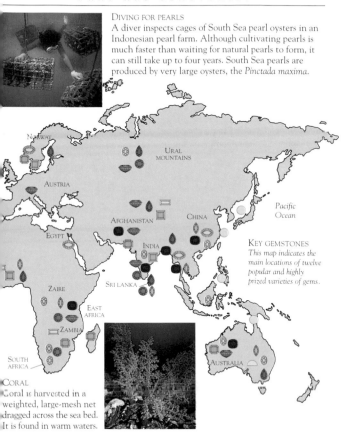

DIVING FOR PEARLS
A diver inspects cages of South Sea pearl oysters in an Indonesian pearl farm. Although cultivating pearls is much faster than waiting for natural pearls to form, it can still take up to four years. South Sea pearls are produced by very large oysters, the *Pinctada maxima*.

NORWAY

URAL
MOUNTAINS

AUSTRIA

Pacific
Ocean

AFGHANISTAN   CHINA

EGYPT

INDIA

KEY GEMSTONES
This map indicates the main locations of twelve popular and highly prized varieties of gems.

ZAIRE   SRI LANKA

EAST
AFRICA

ZAMBIA

SOUTH
AFRICA

AUSTRALIA

CORAL
Coral is harvested in a weighted, large-mesh net dragged across the sea bed. It is found in warm waters.

How gemstones are formed

Mineral gemstones are formed within the Earth as a result of certain physical and chemical conditions. Heat and pressure are the main external factors involved in gemstones' formation. Some are brought to the surface by volcanic eruptions; others are found in rocks or in gem gravels – the deposits left by rivers and streams as they gradually erode rocks.

1 Diamond and pyrope garnet crystallize at high pressures in the Earth's mantle.

2 High pressures in the Earth's crust can lead to the formation of jadeite.

3 Peridot occurs in basaltic and ultrabasic rocks.

4 Chrysoberyl, topaz, aquamarine, tourmaline, quartz, spessartine, and moonstone crystallize when coarse-grained igneous granites (pegmatites) cool down.

5 Emeralds occur when granitic fluids come into contact with rocks containing chromium.

6 Extreme pressure and temperature changes in shale can give rise to the crystallization of ruby, sapphire, chrysoberyl, spinel, and garnet.

PERIDOT

Peridot forms deep beneath the Earth's surface

GRAN

MALACHITE

Malachite often occurs in rounded masses

7 Ruby, sapphire, spinel, zircon, lapis lazuli, spessartine, and grossular garnet form when hot granitic fluids react with impure shales and limestones.

CROSS SECTION OF EARTH

CONTINENTAL CRUST

VOLCANIC CRUST

8 Rising magma carries gem minerals to the Earth's surface, where they are trapped in basalt lavas.

9 Turquoise, malachite, and azurite tend to form close to the Earth's surface, where ore bodies come into contact with water.

10 Opal is found in porous sedimentary rocks and sometimes in cavities in volcanic rocks. It forms during cooling of silica-rich groundwater.

Layer of precious opal

OPAL

11 Silica-rich liquids deposit citrine, amethyst, agate, and opal in gas cavities in lavas.

12 Various weathering processes break down gem-bearing rocks.

13 Gems are washed into river gravels.

Crystal structure

Most gemstones are made up of crystals, which grow in a regular, three-dimensional pattern. Crystals can be classified into seven different systems according to the symmetry of their faces, or flat surfaces. The overall shape formed by the surfaces is called the "habit". Some gemstones have an irregular shape, known as "amorphous".

CHRYSOPRASE

REGULAR STRUCTURE

As with the other members of the chalcedony family, chrysoprase has a trigonal structure (see facing page), which is characterized by a three-fold symmetry.

JET

Fine-grained, rough surface

AMORPHOUS

Jet, along with amber and ivory, is an organic gem that does not fall within the seven crystal systems. Instead, its structure is amorphous, which means literally "without form".

Line of cleavage

CLEAVAGE

The way in which a stone breaks, or cleaves, depends on its planes of weakness. These planes relate to its crystal structure and are usually parallel, perpendicular, or diagonal to the crystal faces.

TOPAZ

CRYSTAL STRUCTURE

AXES OF SYMMETRY
Each crystal system has different axes of symmetry – imaginary lines around which the crystal rotates and still shows the same aspect. The diagrams indicate the minimum number of times a crystal shows the same aspect in each rotation.

SPINEL

CUBIC
Spinel is a typical cubic crystal. The cubic system has the highest symmetry – three four-fold axes.

TRIGONAL
This crystal system has one three-fold axis. It has the same axis of symmetry as the hexagonal.

MILKY QUARTZ

TETRAGONAL
This system is defined by one four-fold axis. Here a zircon displays double pyramidal ends.

ZIRCON

MONOCLINIC
Gems such as malachite, moonstone, and jade belong to the monoclinic system, which has one two-fold axis.

MALACHITE

HEXAGONAL
Emerald and aquamarine belong to this system. They have one six-fold axis of symmetry.

AQUAMARINE

ORTHORHOMBIC
There are a minimum of three two-fold axes in this system.

TOPAZ

TRICLINIC
Triclinic gems are unusual in that they have no axes of symmetry and are therefore the least symmetrical.

TURQUOISE

Physical properties

Mineral gemstones can be identified and classified according to certain properties, ranging from how hard they are to their relative weights. Hardness is measured on a scale of 1 to 10, with diamond being 10. Specific gravity reflects the density of a gem, and carats are used to measure its weight.

AGATE

Tree-like inclusion

ROCK CRYSTAL

MOHS' HARDNESS SCALE

The German mineralogist Friedrich Mohs devised a scale as a means of classifying the relative hardness of minerals. Hardness was defined as the ability to scratch another mineral, so that each mineral on his scale can scratch those below it and be scratched by those above it.

INCLUSIONS

Internal features of gems such as trapped solids, liquids, or gases are called inclusions. These can be invaluable in identifying certain gems. Needle-like inclusions are often present in rock crystal and "landscape" features tend to form in agates, due to iron oxides and hydroxides.

| 1 TALC | 2 GYPSUM | 3 CALCITE |  4 FLUORITE | 5 APATITE |

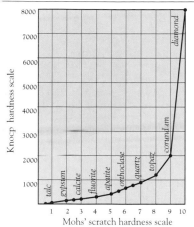

Mohs' scratch hardness scale

(Knoop hardness scale, y-axis; labels: talc, gypsum, calcite, fluorite, apatite, orthoclase, quartz, topaz, corundum, diamond)

SPECIFIC GRAVITY

The density of a gem is called its specific gravity (SG). It is calculated by comparing a stone's weight with the weight of an equal amount of water. The SG of aquamarine, for example, is 2.69, which means it is 2.69 times heavier than an equal amount of water.

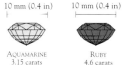

10 mm (0.4 in)	10 mm (0.4 in)
AQUAMARINE 3.15 carats	RUBY 4.6 carats

Ruby has a much higher SG, at 4.00. This means that a 10 mm brilliant-cut ruby will weigh 4.6 carats compared to an aquamarine's 3.15 carats. One carat equals one-fifth of a gram. The word "carat" derives from the carob seed – a standard for weighing gems for centuries.

THE KNOOP HARDNESS SCALE

The intervals between the numbers on Mohs' scale do not represent equal increases in hardness – for example, diamond is four times harder than corundum, but is next to it on the scale. Knoop's scale, instead, reveals the varying degrees of hardness of Mohs' ten minerals.

MOHS' MINERALS

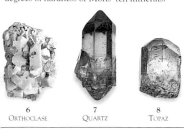

6	7	8	9	10
ORTHOCLASE	QUARTZ	TOPAZ	CORUNDUM	DIAMOND

Colour and lustre

A gemstone's value depends largely on its colour and the way in which it reflects light. The term "lustre" describes the amount of light reflected from the surface of a mineral; gems range from highly lustrous (adamantine) to waxy (low lustre). Their colour depends on how they absorb light, as well as the type and amount of impurities they contain. Some gems occur in only one colour, for example, malachite, which is always green.

SPLITTING LIGHT
White light is made up of all the colours of the rainbow. If a gem appears red, it is because red is reflected back, while the other colours are absorbed.

IDENTIFYING GEMSTONES
Many gems are so similar in colour that it is impossible to tell them apart with the naked eye. Gemmologists use an instrument known as a spectroscope, which separates light into its spectrum of colours. This reveals the way each stone absorbs bands of coloured light. The pattern that each gemstone makes is like its individual "fingerprint".

Red with distinctive banding

RUBY

Red tapering to orange

ALMANDINE GARNET

ABSORPTION SPECTRA   *Broad band of black*

GLASS

PARTI-COLOURED GEMS

Some gemstones are made up of two or more colours. Tourmalines are excellent examples of this, since a single crystal may display as many as 15 different colours or shades. This watermelon tourmaline has three bands of colour.

Lapis with white flecks of calcite

WATERMELON TOURMALINE

IDIOCHROMATIC GEMS

Although the shade may vary, lapis lazuli is always blue. This is due to its sulphur content, which is an essential part of its composition. Gems of this type are known as "idiochromatic", or self-coloured.

Vitreous lustre

Resinous lustre

ADAMANTINE LUSTRE

Diamonds typically have an "adamantine" lustre, which is the highest and most desirable degree of sheen. The brilliant cut is popular for diamonds since it maximizes this effect.

VITREOUS LUSTRE

Malachite has a glass-like quality, known as a vitreous lustre. It is also opaque, i.e. it lets no light through. The characteristic green colour of malachite is caused by its copper content.

RESINOUS LUSTRE

This polished amber bead has a resinous sheen. Amber with less shine than this is often called "waxy".

Adamantine lustre

Cut and polish

Uncut gems often look like
ordinary stones. It is the cutting
and polishing processes that
transform "rocks" into jewels.
Gems may be cut into a number
of flat surfaces, known as facets,
or rounded and
polished into
cabochons.

Marking gem with Indian ink

1 ROUGH
Model of the rough
crystal ready for faceting.

Crown *Girdle*

2 GRIND
The top of the crystal is
sawn off, and the stone
is rounded using a
diamond grinder.

Girdle *Pavilion*

FACETING A GEMSTONE
Decisions on the best style
of cut are reached by careful
examination of a gem's form
and structure. The final
gem may be as little as
40 per cent of the original.

Crown facets

3 CUT
The main
facets are
added to
the crown.

5 FINAL CUT
The standard round brilliant
cut has 58 facets, precisely
angled and in perfect
proportion to each other.

Star facet

Crown facet

4 TOP AND BOTTOM
The eight main crown facets
are completed and facets are
added below the girdle.

REFLECTING LIGHT

The ideal cut maximizes the amount of light that is reflected back from the stone. If a gem cut is too deep or too shallow, the stone will not sparkle.

DEEP CUT
Light is deflected, then escapes through base

Light escapes on opposite side

SHALLOW CUT
Light escapes on same side of base

IDEAL CUT
Light is reflected back and out of the top of the stone

HI-TECH CUTTING

Computers have revolutionized the cutting and polishing processes. This operator oversees the faceting operation on screen.

PRECISION CUTTING

TYPES OF CUT

This table shows the most popular cuts, which are shown for each of the main gemstones featured in this book. Faceted cuts are grouped as brilliant, mixed, step, and fancy. Non-faceted gems are also listed.

BRILLIANT CUTS	Round	Oval			
MIXED CUTS	Mixed	Cushion			
STEP CUTS	Octagonal	Oval	Baguette	Table	Square
FANCY CUTS	Pendeloque	Marquise			
POLISHED/ CAMEO CUTS	Cabochon	Bead	Cameo	Polished	

MINING

THE COLLECTING OF GEMS can be as simple as panning for stones in a river bed, or involve vastly expensive, technologically advanced mining equipment. In some parts of the world, traditional methods are the most cost-effective, but for stones such as diamonds, which are often embedded deep in volcanic rocks, the most modern mining processes have to be used.

PANNING FOR RUBIES
Thai workers pan for rubies using an age-old method. The hardness and weight of rubies allow them to be be sifted from river gravel and then picked out by hand.

PANNING FOR RUBIES IN THAILAND

OPAL MINING IN AUSTRALIA
Opal is often found in sandstone and so can be dislodged relatively easily. Electronic diggers are used underground, and gem-bearing rubble is then sucked up to the surface, where it is sorted.

Hardened sandy clay

MATRIX OPAL
Opal is a silica gel containing a high proportion of water. It forms by filling cavities in a rock and hardening.

GEM TREASURE TROVE

Panning operates on the principle that lighter materials are washed away by the swirling action of water, leaving behind precious minerals. This technique is often used in areas such as Myanmar (Burma).

Precious stones mixed in with other minerals

SOUTH AFRICAN DIAMOND MINE

The scale of a diamond-mining operation is astounding, in terms of both the size of the pit and the amount of equipment needed. Over 250 tonnes of rock have to be blasted for every finished diamond carat, i.e., for each .2 g (0.007 oz)!

TRAWLING FOR DIAMONDS

The seabed off the Namibian coast is an important source of diamonds. The latest recovery technique involves large, offshore ships that pump gravel containing diamonds up to the surface.

ORGANICS

GEMS THAT ARE THE PRODUCTS of plants and animals, rather than having a mineral origin, are known as organics. Pearls, coral, and amber come into this category, as do ivory, jet, and different types of shell. These materials have been prized and used as ornaments for thousands of years.

JAPANESE PEARL DIVER

CORAL
Coral grows in warm waters at depths of 3–300 m (10–1,000 ft). Its tree-like branches tend to be dull and grainy when harvested, but can be polished to a high lustre.

CORAL BE

FISHING FOR PEARLS   *Pearl in oyster*
Japan pioneered the development of cultured pearls at the turn of the 20th century, and it now dominates the world pearl market. Here a diver swims with a large bucket to gather specially farmed *akoya* oysters, with their valuable pearls.

CORAL REE

FOSSILIZED JEWEL
Organic gems are softer than mineral gemstones and tend to be less durable. Jet is 2.5 on Mohs' scale of hardness, the same as a fingernail. It is fossilized wood, a product of trees that lived millions of years ago, and has been used decoratively since the Bronze Age.

FOSSILIZED
WOOD

JET BEAD

CARVED IVORY

IVORY
Elephants' tusks have long been the main source of ivory, but are by no means the only one. The teeth and tusks of many other mammals also contain ivory and are now often used in preference to elephant ivory, since elephants are a protected species. Ivory is prized for its colour, ease of carving, and durability.

Elephant tusks

AMBER
Like jet, amber is a fossil derived from trees, but in this case from the resin rather than the compacted remains of the wood. It is characteristically a golden orange colour and this, coupled with its translucence and resinous lustre, have made it popular for jewellery.

Fossilized resin from pine tree

TORTOISESHELL
The term "tortoiseshell" is confusing, since it refers to the carapace (upper shell) of a hawksbill turtle rather than that of a tortoise. It was extremely popular for hair ornaments and small boxes in the early part of this century, but is now a protected substance.

TORTOISESHELL

Resinous lustre

AMBER BEAD

Turtle with tortoiseshell carapace

HAWKSBILL TURTLE

ARTIFICIAL GEMS

THE DEMAND FOR RARE GEMSTONES has led
to the production of countless imitations,
some more successful than others. These
copies fall into three categories: gems that
look like the real thing, but have a different
composition; synthetic gems, which are made
in laboratories and are almost exact copies of
natural gems; and composite stones, which
consist of several parts cemented together.

FLAME-FUSION TECHNIQUE

In 1891, the French scientist August Verneuil
perfected a technique for producing synthetic
gems. He sifted powdered crystals into a flame
(left), and melted them onto a holder. The
melted crystal was then removed from the heat,
and it formed a solid crystal (right, top section).

FLAME FUSION

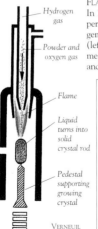

Hydrogen gas

Powder and oxygen gas

Flame

Liquid turns into solid crystal rod

Pedestal supporting growing crystal

VERNEUIL TECHNIQUE

GROWING CRYSTALS

Many crystals grow in hot fluids as they cool down.
Although this process can be replicated in a
laboratory, it takes many years to produce gem-quality
crystals in this way, and so is not commercially viable.

STUBBY CRYSTALS START TO FORM

CRYSTALS BEGIN TO TAKE SHAPE

SYNTHETIC EMERALD

This pendeloque-cut emerald has been made by the flux-melt technique (see page 17). Its composition and structure are the same as that of a natural emerald.

Synthetic emerald

COMPOSITE STONE

Red garnet on top of green glass

IDENTIFYING GEMS

It is usually possible to distinguish between real and artificial gems with a small hand lens, called a loupe. This one has ten-fold magnification.

HAND-HELD LENS

GARNET-TOPPED EMERALD DOUBLET

This composite stone is made of a red garnet top and a green glass base. It appears green despite the garnet and is intended to pass for an emerald. The garnet-topped doublet is a common composite stone.

GILSON OPAL

OPAL

The French manufacturer Gilson has imitated the opal's iridescence. However, these opals have patches of colour and are not perfect replicas.

FABULOUS FAKE

This pendant is made up of simulated rubies and diamonds, probably glass. The gems are imitation rather than synthetic, as they do not have the same chemical composition as real stones.

Simulated rubies, probably glass

RUBY AND DIAMOND PENDANT

Fake diamonds

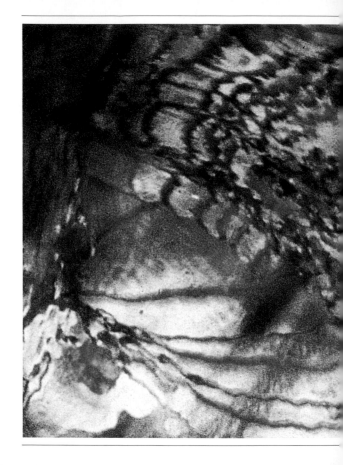

COLOUR
KEY

INTRODUCTION

THE MAJORITY OF GEMS are coloured by metallic elements, notably chromium, iron, manganese, titanium, and copper. Depending on the type and amount of metal contained in a gemstone, its colour can vary greatly. In this section, gemstones are categorized according to seven basic colour bands.

Intense red in ruby is caused by chromium

Yellow sapphires contain iron

Green sapphires are often made up of microscopic bands of yellow and blue sapphire

MULTI-COLOURED
These rubies and sapphires belong to the same mineral, corundum. The range of colours is caused by varying amounts of chromium, iron, and titanium.

Prized blue sapphires contain titanium with iron

PAINT PIGMENTS

Azurite is a copper compound that produces a sky-blue colour when ground down. Malachite produces a brilliant green, and lapis lazuli generates the beautiful and highly prized blue known as ultramarine.

MALACHITE

AZURITE

LAPIS LAZULI

COLOURLESS

ALWAYS COLOURLESS

ROCK CRYSTAL
(Quartz p. 74–5)

ACHROITE
(Tourmaline p. 70–1)

IMITATION
DIAMONDS
Cubic zirconia
Strontium titanate
Glass

USUALLY COLOURLESS

DIAMOND
(p. 50–3)

OTHER GEMS
Scheelite
Celestine
Danburite
Cerussite

ORTHOCLASE
(Moonstone family p. 84–5)

SOMETIMES COLOURLESS

ZIRCON
(p. 68–9)

MOONSTONE
(p. 84–5)

SAPPHIRE
(p. 56–7)

RED OR PINK

ALWAYS RED OR PINK

PINK GROSSULAR
(Garnet p. 72–3)

RUBY
(p. 54–5)

ALMANDINE
(Garnet p. 72–3)

USUALLY RED OR PINK

PYROPE
(Garnet p. 72–3)

RUBELLITE
(Tourmaline p. 70–1)

SPESSARTINE
(Garnet p. 72–3)

SOMETIMES RED OR PINK

TOPAZ
(p. 62–3)

WATERMELON TOURMALINE
(p. 70–1)

SAPPHIRE
(p. 56–7)

CORAL
(p. 98–9)

SPINEL
(p. 60–1)

JADEITE
(Jade p. 80–1)

WHITE OR SILVER

ALWAYS WHITE OR SILVER

IVORY
(p. 102–3)

DONKEY'S-EAR ABALONE
(Shell p. 106–7)

MILKY QUARTZ
(p. 74–5)

USUALLY WHITE OR SILVER

SOMETIMES WHITE OR SILVER

PEARL
(p. 96–7)

SHELL
(p. 106–7)

NEPHRITE
(Jade p. 80–1)

YELLOW–BROWN

ALWAYS YELLOW–BROWN

PADPARADSCHA
(Sapphire p. 56–7)

CARNELIAN
(Chalcedony p. 78–9)

FIRE OPAL
(p. 86–7)

SARDONYX
(Chalcedony p. 78–9)

HESSONITE
(Garnet p. 72–3)

DRAVITE
(Tourmaline p. 70–1)

TORTOISESHELL
(Shell p. 106–7)

CITRINE
(Quartz p. 74–5)

OTHER GEMS
Heliodor
Sunstone
Cassiterite
Smoky quartz

OTHER GEMS
Vesuvianite
Titanite
Axinite
Staurolite

ORTHOCLASE
(*Moonstone family p. 84–5*)

AMBER
(*p. 104–5*)

SPESSARTINE
(*Garnet p. 72–3*)

CHRYSOBERYL
(*p. 58–9*)

CHATOYANT QUARTZ
(*Chalcedony p. 78–9*)

MOSS AGATE
(*Chalcedony p. 78–9*)

CAT'S EYE
(*Chalcedony p. 78–9*)

SAPPHIRE
(*p. 56–7*)

GREEN

ALWAYS GREEN

EMERALD
(p. 64–5)

PERIDOT
(p. 82–3)

BLOODSTONE
(Chalcedony p. 78–9)

UVAROVITE
(Garnet p. 72–3)

CHRYSOPRASE
(Chalcedony p. 78–9)

MALACHITE
(p. 92–3)

USUALLY GREEN

JADEITE
(Jade p. 80–1)

NEPHRITE
(Jade p. 80–1)

DEMANTOID
(Garnet p. 72–3)

SOMETIMES GREEN

AGATE
(*Chalcedony* p. 78–9)

SAPPHIRE
(p. 56–7)

WATERMELON TOURMALINE
(p. 70–1)

DIAMOND
(p. 50–1)

OTHER GEMS
Paua Shell
Fluorite
Smithsonite
Euclase
Kyanite

ZIRCON
(p. 68–9)

GROSSULAR GARNET
(*Garnet* p. 72–3)

GARNET-TOPPED DOUBLET
(p. 72–3)

TOURMALINE
(p. 70–1)

BLUE OR VIOLET

ALWAYS BLUE OR VIOLET

AQUAMARINE
(p. 66–7)

TURQUOISE
(p. 88–9)

AZURITE
(p. 92–3)

LAPIS LAZULI
(p. 90–1)

AMETHYST
(p. 76–7)

HAUYNE
(*Lapis lazuli p. 90–1*)

SOMETIMES BLUE OR VIOLET

TOPAZ
(p. 62–3)

SAPPHIRE
(p. 56–7)

SPINEL
(p. 60–1)

BLACK

ALWAYS BLACK

JET
(p. 100–1)

SCHORL
(Tourmaline p. 70–1)

ARTIFICIAL JET
Cannel coal
Vulcanized
rubber
Glass

SOMETIMES BLACK

CORAL
(p. 98–9)

DIAMOND
(p. 50–1)

PEARL
(p. 96–7)

IRIDESCENT

OPAL
(p. 86–7)

FIRE AGATE
(Chalcedony p. 78–9)

MOTHER-OF-PEARL
(Shell p. 106–7)

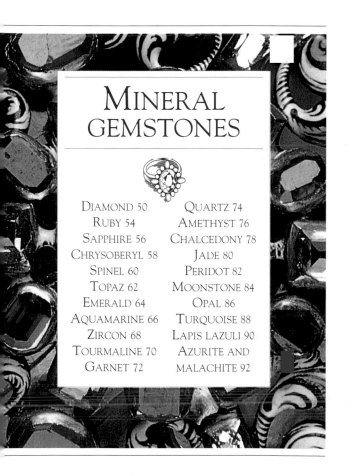

MINERAL GEMSTONES

DIAMOND

KNOWN AS THE "king of gems", the diamond is the most precious of gemstones, famed both for its fiery brilliance and for being the hardest mineral on earth. Its name derives from the Greek word *adamas*, which means "invincible". Diamonds are a form of carbon. They occur in a range of colours, the most popular being colourless.

DIAMOND IN MATRIX
Diamonds are sometimes found in conglomerate rock, as shown here. It is a solidified mixture of pebbles and grains.

MYTH AND MAGIC

• Hindus believed that a flawed diamond would bring misfortune.

• The Greeks thought that diamonds could protect against poisons.

• In medieval times, those who could afford to wore a diamond jewel to safeguard against the plague.

PENDANT

PEARL AND DIAMOND PENDANT
In the Victorian era, sporting diamond jewellery was one of the favourite ways of displaying wealth. This piece dates from the 1850s.

Diamond weighs 2.48 carats

ENGAGEMENT RING
Diamonds, symbols of love and fidelity, have been used in engagement rings since the 15th century.

Brilliant Cushion Pendeloque

HARDNESS 10

DIAMOND NECKLACE
This necklace containing
diamond loops and festoons dates
from about 1870. The diamonds
are brilliants of varying sizes.

NECKLACE

*Brilliant cut
is typical for
diamonds*

COLOURED DIAMONDS
The gem-quality, coloured
stones pictured right are called
fancies and fetch a very high price. Traces of
nitrogen give brown, yellow, green,
and black stones; boron is
present in blue
diamonds.

Champagne

Black

Silver

Green

Purple

Rose

Gold

FANCIES

BUTTERFLY
BROOCH

*Brilliant-cut
diamonds*

DIAMOND
BRACELET

*Flexible
links*

BUTTERFLY
Dating from about 1860, this delicate
openwork brooch consists of over 125
brilliant-cut diamonds. The ruby
eyes form a striking contrast to the
shimmering white wings.

BRACELET
Designed with
flexible-band links,
this diamond-studded
bracelet dates from
the late 19th century.

Famous diamonds

The history of diamonds is one of untold greed, intrigue, and deceit. Countries have been plundered for them, wars fought, and beautiful women lost and won. However, not all diamonds have brought about such destruction. The Taylor–Burton diamond, for example, was used to save lives: in 1978, it was sold to finance a hospital in Botswana.

TAYLOR–BURTON
The actor Richard Burton bought this pear-shaped diamond for his wife Elizabeth Taylor in 1969. Nine years later they divorced, and she put it up for auction.

Gem cut from a rough stone of 241 carats

DRESDEN GREEN
Known as the Dresden Green, this is the largest green diamond in existence, measuring roughly 30 x 20 x 10mm (7.5 x 5 x 2.5 in) and weighing 41 carats.

CULLINAM 1
Also known as the Great Star of Africa, this stone was found in South Africa's Premier Mine in 1905. It took three polishers, working 14 hours a day, eight months to cut and polish it! Presented to King Edward VII in 1908, it is now set within the British Imperial Sceptre.

THE TIFFANY
This diamond was bought by Tiffany's, the New York jeweller, in 1879 for $18,000. Just over 100 years later, it was valued at $12 million.

Largest known yellow diamond

THE SANCY
In the 16th century, the Sancy was used to finance a war in Europe. The servant bearing it swallowed the stone when attacked. The stone was later retrieved from his stomach!

THE HOPE
Despite its name, owners of the Hope Diamond are said to be cursed. One was eaten by wild beasts; Louis XVI of France was guillotined; a Dutch jeweller committed suicide; an actress was shot on stage while wearing it; and her lover, whose gift it was, was stabbed to death!

KOH-I-NOOR
The Koh-i-noor passed rapidly from owner to owner – Indian, Moghul, and Persian. It was presented to Queen Victoria in 1850 and was set in the crown worn by Her Majesty the Queen Mother in 1937.

Koh-i-noor Diamond set in Maltese cross

RUBY

THE CLASSIC RUBY is a deep, rich red, although the stone can appear in shades from pink to purple to brown, depending on the chemical content. Rubies are second only to diamonds in terms of hardness, and this, along with the vibrancy of their colour, makes them highly prized for jewellery. Like sapphires, they are a form of corundum, and the finest stones come from Myanmar (Burma).

Five rubies hang within a diamond border

A typical cut for rubies

CUSHION MIXED CUT
Mixed-cut stones usually have a rounded outline, with the upper section cut as brilliants and the lower section step cut. Rubies are usually cut this way.

GEORGIAN DROPS
Diamonds are often used to set off the colour of the ruby, as in these earrings dating from c.1800.

Brilliant   Step   Cabochon   Mixed

HARDNESS 9

EDWARDIAN PENDANT
The pale tones of this ruby suggest that it was mined in Sri Lanka. Hindus considered light-coloured rubies "female" gems, and the darker ones "male".

FLORAL SPRAY
This brooch is set with circular rubies, step-cut diamonds, and a large brilliant-cut diamond at the centre.

Pale ruby cut en cabochon

Deep red mixed-cut rubies

RUBY PENDANT

CLASSIC RING
Traditionally given as 40th-wedding anniversary presents, rubies are also the gemstones of those born in July.

Six-rayed star

MYTH AND MAGIC
• At the time of the Borgias (15th–16th centuries), rubies were thought to counteract poison – and so were much in demand!

• Rubbed on the skin, these gemstones were once thought to restore youth and vitality.

• In the Middle Ages, the ruby was viewed as a stone of prophecy. People believed it would darken when its wearer was in danger.

STAR RUBY
The colour of this cabochon is known as "pigeon's-blood red" – pure red with a hint of blue – and is the most sought-after shade.

SAPPHIRE

THESE STONES come in a range of yellows, pinks, and greens, as well as the better-known blue variety. The deep blue "heavenly" sapphires were, and to some extent still are, deemed holy: popes, cardinals, and bishops have worn them since the Middle Ages. They are known as the jewels of chastity.

Diamonds

SHIMMERING BROOCH
In its purest form the sapphire is colourless; traces of vanadium render it violet. Here the clarity of the diamonds enhances the tones of the central sapphire.

RING
The unusual colour of this sapphire ring is due to the presence of a small amount of iron.

MYTH AND MAGIC

• At one time sapphires were thought to exude heavenly rays that had the power to kill all poisonous creatures.

• The Persians thought the earth rested on a giant sapphire and that the blue of the heavens was its reflection.

GREEN CUSHION CUT
Sapphires from Australia and the US state of Montana are often of a dark green hue.

Brilliant

Cabochon

Cameo

Brilliant

Cushion

HARDNESS 9

LATE VICTORIAN NECKLACE
The stones in this intricate necklace are of a pale blue variety. Blue sapphires derive their colour from mixtures of iron and traces of titanium, while green varieties are due to greater quantities of iron, and pink to the presence of chromium.

Diamond quatrefoils form links

Brilliant-cut sapphire

The sapphire and diamond drop is detachable

STAR CABOCHON
Star sapphires were considered the most potent of amulets. The three intersecting arms were said to represent faith, hope, and destiny.

SAPPHIRE EARRINGS
These delicate sapphire and diamond drop earrings date from about 1890. The cabochons are of highly prized cornflower blue and probably come from Sri Lanka.

Diamond-set leaves

Cabochon cut

OVAL MIXED CUT
Like rubies, pink sapphires are thought to ward off ill health and misfortune, particularly when worn on the skin.

CHRYSOBERYL

THE NAME "CHRYSOBERYL" comes from the stone's beryllium content plus the Greek *chrysos*, meaning "golden". Interesting types are alexandrite, which can change from green to red, mauve, or brown, depending on the light, and cat's-eye, which looks as it sounds and allegedly protects against the "evil eye".

Characteristic wedge-shaped ends

CRYSTALS
The best chrysoberyl has been found in the Ural Mountains of western Russia. Other rich sources are Sri Lanka, Zimbabwe, Tanzania, and Brazil.

Gold filigree setting

BROOCH
At 8.5 on Mohs' scale, chrysoberyl is one of the hardest stones and so is particularly prized for jewellery. This Victorian piece is made of over 20 individual mixed-cut stones.

Mixed-cut gems

CUSHION MIXED CUT
Here hundreds of facets reflect the golden colour for which chrysoberyl is renowned. Despite the stone's brilliance, it is thought to lack "fire".

Brilliant

Cushion

Cabochon

Mixed

HARDNESS 8.5

ALEXANDRITE
Discovered in 1830
in the emerald
mines of the Urals,
this variety of
chrysoberyl was
named in honour of
Tsar Alexander II.
The stone changes
from green to light
red in artificial light.

NECKLACE
This early 19th-
century necklace
consists of pale,
honey-coloured
chrysoberyls in
a cannetille setting –
an embroidery term
for gold thread with
a spiral twist.

SPANISH DESIGN
The chrysoberyl in this
18th-century ring was
collected from a vein
running through chalk.
The pale yellow stones
are a classic cushion cut
and the large oval ring
is probably of Spanish
or Portuguese origin.

*Filigree work
in palmette
motif*

*Pale yellow
stones*

*Near-white line
across the centre*

CAT'S-EYE

ART DECO RING
Cat's-eye
chrysoberyl
is also known
as cymophane.
It is always cut
en cabochon, and
its value increases
in proportion to the
narrowness and intensity
of its flash of light.

MYTH
AND MAGIC

• In the East, cat's-
eyes are used to
ward off evil spirits.
In the West, they are
used in crystal healing

• Cat's eyes are also
used medicinally in
India, particularly as
a remedy for cancer.

SPINEL

THE COLOUR VARIATIONS of spinel – blue, yellow, and red – are caused by various metallic impurities. The most popular spinel is a ruby red, which contains chromiun and iron. Many treasures of state throughout the world sport massive red spinels, mistaken for rubies. The British Imperial State Crown is no exception.

Diamond surround

DROP EARRINGS
Large pendeloque-cut spinels hang from diamond frames. These earrings form part of an 18th-century jewellery set, which includes a tiara, necklace, and hair ornament.

MYTH AND MAGIC
• Spinel was recognized as a mineral only 150 years ago. Prior to this, it was classified as a ruby and so shared the ruby's reputed medicinal and prophetic powers.

• It was used as a remedy for haemorrhages.

OCTAGONAL STEP CUT
This pink spinel comes from Myanmar (Burma), a rich source of river gravel deposits.

| Cushion | Mixed | Step | Brilliant |

HARDNESS 8

BRITISH
IMPERIAL
STATE
CROWN

BRITISH CROWN
The Black Prince's Ruby is
the spinel in the centre of the
British Imperial State Crown. It
was a gift from Pedro the Cruel,
king of Spain, to the Black
Prince, son of Edward III of
England, in 1367 for his
help in battle.

BRITISH
IMPERIAL
STATE
CROWN

Black Prince's Ruby

OVAL BRILLIANT CUT
Pure spinel is
colourless. This
stone has a pinkish
mauve tinge due to
small amounts of
impurities. Liquid-
filled inclusions
are visible.

MIXED-CUT RED SPINEL
Until the 19th century, red
spinels were known as Balas
rubies, possibly named after
their source, Balascia, now
Badakhshan, in Afghanistan.

Gahnospinel

BLUE SPINEL
This blue,
zinc-rich variety
of spinel is called
gahnospinel, after the
Swedish chemist J. G. Gahn.

TOPAZ

THE NAME "TOPAZ" is thought to come from the Sanskrit *tapas*, meaning "fire". The stone occurs naturally in a range of different colours and is also heat-treated to produce the more popular hues. Pink topaz, for example, is usually an irradiated form of the more common yellow.

ANTIQUE PENDANT
Pink topaz, peridot, and diamonds sparkle from this Victorian pendant, dating from about 1880.

OCTAGONAL STEP CUT
Although blue topaz does occur naturally, it can also be created by heat-treating a colourless variety.

STEP CUT

Foil-backed gems

NECKLACE
The gemstones in this antique necklace are foil-backed to enhance their colour.

The Brazilian Princess weighs over 21,000 carats, or 4 kg (8.8 lb)

PRICELESS
The Brazilian Princess was once the largest gem ever faceted. It is now on display in the Smithsonian Institution in Washington, D. C.

Brilliant	Cushion	Step	Mixed	Pendeloque

HARDNESS 8

PENDELOQUE CUT
It is possible to see tear-shaped inclusions within this cut crystal. They are characteristic of topaz and generally contain bubbles of gas or liquid.

Pink topaz

Diamonds

BROOCH
A large mixed-cut topaz forms the heart of this early 19th-century brooch, framed by 18 cushion-cut diamonds. The outer edge has four more topazes set within diamond foliage.

Brazilian crystal

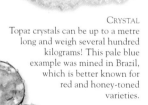

CRYSTAL
Topaz crystals can be up to a metre long and weigh several hundred kilograms! This pale blue example was mined in Brazil, which is better known for red and honey-toned varieties.

OVAL MIXED CUT
Colour is more important than size in determining the value of topaz. Today, pink, blue, and honey-coloured stones are the most sought after.

Honey-coloured gem

MYTH AND MAGIC
• In 1255, St Hildegard offered a simple remedy for failing eyesight: steep a topaz in wine for three days and then lightly rub it over the eyes.

• Worn around the neck, topaz was thought to cure madness.

TOPAZ NECKLACE

EMERALD

THE BEAUTIFUL GREEN SHADES of the emerald derive from the presence of chromium and vanadium. Only the finest quality gemstones are transparent and flawless, most have tiny fractures or mineral inclusions known as a "jardin", the French for garden. It is common practice to oil emerald to disguise these flaws and enhance the colour.

ART DECO RING
A square cut emphasizes the richness of the colour by leading the eye into the stone rather than deflecting attention away from it.

Excellent emerald-green colour

A band of emeralds shows the skeletal structure

SYNTHETIC PENDELOQU[E]
In the 193[0]
American scientis[t]
Carroll Chatha[m]
greatly improved t[he]
process for produci[ng]
synthetic emeralds. H[e]
brewed emerald se[ed]
crystals at extrem[e]
temperatures for [a]
to a ye[ar]

Insects were popular motifs in Victorian jewellery

GRASSHOPPER BROOCH
Lush green emeralds are symbolic of the freshness of nature, and the choice of a grass-hopper for this emerald-studded brooch adds to that symbolism.

 Pendeloque

Step

 Step

Cabocho[n]

HARDNESS 7–8

ANTIQUE CABOCHON EARRINGS
These Art Deco earrings boast large hanging emeralds. Inclusions – marks either on or within the surface of the stone – are clearly visible, and the carving draws the eye around the surface of the gem rather than into it.

Polished oval cabochons are framed in black enamel

This gem is larger and lighter in colour than the other one

Inclusions provide keys to the gem's origins

OCTAGONAL CABOCHON
Emeralds almost always have fissures or inclusions. These may be embedded crystals of other materials, growth lines, or any of a whole range of microscopic occurrences. They tell the story of the gem's origin millions of years ago.

POLISHED PEBBLE
Not all emeralds have to be prised out of rocks. Some find their way into river gravels, where the action of the water tumbles and smooths them so that they resemble shiny pebbles.

MYTH AND MAGIC
• Hundreds of years ago, emeralds were thought to possess healing powers, particularly for restoring eyesight.

• During the Renaissance, emeralds were exchanged among the aristocracy as symbols – and tests – of friendship; the stone would stay intact only if the friendship lasted.

AQUAMARINE

THE SEAWATER COLOUR of aquamarine has given this gemstone its name. In the 19th century, sea-green varieties were the most popular, but blues are more valued today. There are deposits in most continents, although the best quality aquamarines come from Brazil.

PRECIOUS RING
This early 20th-century ring is step cut to reveal its flawless internal structure. It weighs nearly 21 carats and is worth many thousands of dollars.

BRILLIANT CUT
Depending on the angle at which an aquamarine is viewed, it may appear blue, green, or colourless. This so-called "pleochroic" effect is enhanced by many small facets.

MYTH AND MAGIC

• In medieval times, this stone was thought to reawaken the love of married couples. It was also believed to render soldiers invincible.

• Aquamarine is known as the sailor's gem, ensuring safe passage across stormy seas.

CABOCHON
The combination of a cabochon cut and growth lines within the crystal structure create this cat's-eye effect. Six-rayed stars are also sometimes visible.

Fibrous habit contributes to cat's-eye effect

Brilliant   Step   Cabochon

HARDNESS 7–8

OCTAGONAL STEP CUT
Heat-treatment may enhance
or alter the colour of a
gemstone and is considered
perfectly acceptable. With
aquamarine, it tends to change
the hue from green to blue.
This untreated stone has a
distinctive greenish tinge.

*Untreated
stone has
greenish hue*

*The layers of
facets are
clearly visible*

UNTREATED, SKY-BLUE STONE
Large crystals of aquamarine are
relatively common. In 1910, one was found
in Brazil weighing 110.5 kg (243 lb), twice
the weight of an average woman!

*Diamonds
set off the
pale blue
aquamarines*

*Brilliant-
cut outer
stones*

CARTIER BROOCH
Designed by the renowned
French jewellers Cartier, this Art
Deco aquamarine and diamond
brooch dates from about 1930. The
two central stones are step cut.

*Unusual
pendeloque-cut
drop earrings*

ZIRCON

IN THEIR PUREST FORM, zircons are colourless, but more commonly they are golden brown. The name "zircon" is thought to come from the Persian *zargun*, meaning "golden". Although they occur in a range of colours, many zircons are heat-treated to produce the popular blue or colourless varieties.

Brilliant cut enhances colour

Brown zircon can turn blue when heated

ZIRCON PEBBLES
Gem-quality crystals are usually found as brown pebbles in alluvial deposits in places such as Sri Lanka and Myanmar (Burma). Those on the right have been heat-treated.

GOLDEN BROWN
These earrings display the distinctive golden tones of zircons. The brilliant cut adds to their natural fire.

HEAT-TREATED ZIRCON

BAGUETTE CUT
This colourless stone started its life as a reddish-brown zircon crystal.

BLUE ZIRCON RING
This step-cut zircon is set in a four-claw mount with white gold. It was made in the late 1930s.

Brilliant   Cushion   Baguette   Mixed

HARDNESS 7.5

COLOURLESS ZIRCON RING

Clear zircons are frequently sold, intentionally or mistakenly, as diamonds. Zircons display a similar fire to diamonds, but are brittle and susceptible to damage, particularly around the edges of the stone.

Zircons cut as rose diamonds

GREEN ZIRCON NECKLACE

In this early 20th-century necklace, 36 step-cut stones are set in silver-gilt mounts to protect them and heighten their colour and shine.

Step-cut zircons

Silver-gilt mounts

BROOCH

The zircons in this floral brooch are naturally colourless. The danger of using heat-treated stones is that under certain conditions they can revert to their original hue.

Indian-style silver setting

CUSHION BRILLIANT CUT

In Roman times, golden stones were the most popular and prized. The impurities in zircons can also produce green, blue, red, and yellow varieties.

MYTH AND MAGIC

• Zircons that lost their lustre were once thought to be a sign of danger.

• All zircons were deemed magical. In the 14th century, they were popularly worn to safeguard against the Black Death.

TOURMALINE

USUALLY OCCURRING as long, three-sided prisms, tourmalines come in a vast range of colours and an equally large range of varieties. For example, rubellite is red-toned, indicolite is dark blue, and achroite is colourless. Important tourmaline deposits are found in Brazil, California, and the Russian Federation.

Ornate carvings

CHINESE BOTTLE
A pheasant, symbol of prosperity and good fortune, is carved into the tourmaline. This ornate bottle was designed to hold snuff.

ACHROITE
These rare tourmalines are named after the Greek word *achroos*, meaning "without colour".

STEP-CUT RUBELLITE
In 1777, King Gustavus III of Sweden presented a deep red tourmaline to the Russian Empress Catherine the Great, believing it to be a priceless ruby.

Cushion   Cameo   Brilliant   Step

MUSEUM PIECES
These earrings are copies of an early 19th-century design. The originals would probably have been made with emeralds. Green tourmaline is fairly common and is known as verdelite.

Verdelite tourmaline

Brilliant cut

WATERMELON TOURMALINE
Many tourmaline crystals are multicoloured. The watermelon variety is rarely used in jewellery.

DRAVITE
Dark brown tourmalines are rich in magnesium. They can be lightened by heat-treatment.

Cushion mixed-cut dravite

SCHORL
Black tourmalines are very common. They used to be popular for mourning jewellery during Victorian times.

Schorl is rich in iron

SCHORL CRYSTAL

Domed tourmaline

PURPLE PENDANT
Held by a diamond-studded "ribbon", this domed purple tourmaline is exceptionally large, measuring 37 mm (1.5 in) across.

MYTH AND MAGIC
• In the 18th century, a Dutch scientist claimed that a tourmaline wrapped in silk and placed against the cheek of a feverish child would induce sleep.

GARNET

A NUMBER OF GEMSTONES sharing a similar cubic crystal structure and chemical composition make up the garnet family. The colour of these varies greatly, although the name garnet comes from the Latin for pomegranate, which has bright red, garnet-like seeds.

Unusual rounded pendeloques

VICTORIAN EARRINGS
The gold design on these drop earrings represents the arms and neck of an amphora (a Greek or Roman storage vessel).

Circular and pear-shaped stones

MYTH AND MAGIC
• In medieval times, garnets were thought to cure depression, protect against bad dreams, and relieve diseases of the liver and haemorrhages.

• According to legend, Noah used a finely cut, glowing garnet to illuminate the ark.

PYROPE
Of the red garnets, pyrope and almandine are the two most popular for jewellery. The blood-red colour of the pyrope is due to its iron and chromium content.

Brilliant

Step

Cabochon

Mixed

SPESSARTINE
It is rare to find gem-quality spessartine, and this example has characteristic inclusions.

Liquid inclusions

Brilliant cut enhances violet colour

ALMANDINE
Almandine tends to have a violet tint. As well as its use in jewellery, almandine was once incorporated in church and temple stained-glass windows.

Green demantoid garnets

LIZARD BROOCH
In Europe, the lizard is often regarded as a love charm and is a symbol of renewal. Here demantoids, the most valuable of the garnet family, form the body.

GARNET
NECKLACE
Dating from about 1820, this necklace has a flower motif with rosette clusters and decorative leaves set in gold.

QUARTZ

ROCK CRYSTAL, ROSE QUARTZ, and citrine all belong to the quartz family. Rock crystal is the purest of these; its name derives from *krustallos*, the Greek word for ice, as the stone was originally thought to be a type of ice created by the gods. Rose quartz is rose-tinted, caused by traces of titanium; citrine is a golden version of quartz and is coloured by its iron content.

Faceted rock crystal

CRYSTAL BEADS
Rock crystal beads come in a variety of shapes and finishes. They may be carved, frosted, or, as here, faceted and highly polished.

CHINESE BOTTLE
This crystal snuff bottle dates from about 1800. The design incorporates a dragon carved in relief on each side. In China, dragons represent the highest spiritual power.

FLOWER BROOCH
The carving in this piece is typical of work produced in Germany in the 1920s and 1930s. Rock crystal has been carved into a flower head and then frosted, with a diamond at the centre.

Gold leaf

CRYSTAL BROOCH

CRYSTAL BOTTLE

Bead   Cameo   Brilliant

Crystals are typically cloudy

ROSE CRYSTALS

Pink or peach-coloured quartz is known as rose quartz. It tends to be cloudy, and certain varieties produce a star effect when cut *en cabochon*. In ancient Rome, the stone was popular for making seals.

ROSE-TINTED EARRINGS

Pale pink flower heads are framed by silver leaves in these contemporary British earrings. Rose quartz tends to be brittle, so larger carvings may show cracks. It is also prone to fading over

Carved crystal

ROSE QUARTZ

Faceted beads

GOLDEN BEADS

Citrine's name derives from its colour – *citron* being the French for lemon. Gem quality citrine is extremely rare. Large pieces may be carved as pendants; smaller ones, made into beads.

CITRINE NECKLACE

CITRINE DROPS

The best citrine is mined in Brazil, although many of the stones sold as citrines today are in fact heat-treated amethysts. At 470° C (878° F), amethysts produce pale yellow stones. At higher temperatures, the yellow becomes darker.

AMETHYST

OCCURRING IN shades of purple, lilac, and mauve, this is the most valuable of the quartz group. Some amethyst is heat-treated to produce the yellow variety of quartz, known as citrine. Amethyst is traditionally thought to have strong talismanic properties; amethyst crystals are still used in forms of natural healing.

AMETHYST
GRAPES
BROOCH

GRAPES
In myth, Bacchus, Roman god of wine, caused a maiden named Amethyst to be turned into rock crystal. In horror at what he had done, he threw down his goblet of wine, colouring the crystal a beautiful violet.

AMETHYST CRYSTAL AND ROCK CRYSTAL
Here amethyst crystals grow from a bed of rock crystal. Structurally, amethyst is simply a coloured – i.e. containing impurities – form of rock crystal. The colour is often darker at the end of the crystal.

Characteristic pyramid formation

CABOCHON CUFFLINK
These cabochons are notable for their hexagonal cut; most cabochons are either round or oval.

Baguette

Bead

Mixed

7 6

HARDNESS

DROP EARRINGS
These elegant earrings consist of pendeloque-cut amethysts. Generally, deep-coloured stones are faceted to accentuate their colour, while paler or poorer quality ones are cut into cabochons.

Pale-coloured amethyst

MIXED-CUT RING
Amethysts owe their colour to the presence of iron, and deep tones tend to be the most favoured. Rich sources of good-quality crystals come from Russia's Ural Mountains, Brazil, and Uruguay.

Delicate diamond frame

VICTORIAN NECKLACE
The stones of this necklace appear darker than their natural colour because they are backed and surrounded by gold. In the early 19th century, it was not uncommon to place foil behind gemstones in order to enhance their colour.

Enclosed gold setting

FLORAL SPRAY
Nine dark purple crystals have been carved into delicate petals, each flower being made of a single stone inlaid with a central diamond. The brooch is mounted in platinum and 18K gold and is signed by its American designer, William Ruser.

Five petals carved from a single stone

MYTH AND MAGIC
• Amethysts were thought to induce a sober mind; the name is derived from the Greek word *amethystos*, which means "against drunkenness".

• In traditional Chinese medicine, ground amethyst is prescribed for stomach pains and bad dreams.

CHALCEDONY

THE GROUP OF QUARTZES that includes agate, chrysoprase, carnelian, jasper, and bloodstone makes up the family of gemstones known as "chalcedony". They are linked by their microcrystalline structure and waxy or dull appearance. Apple-green chrysoprase is the most valuable of these and has been mined since the 14th century.

Athena, Greek goddess of wisdom and war

Opaque stone

SARDONYX CAMEO RING
Layer stones such as this make ideal material for cameos. Here the white has been carved away to reveal a helmeted Athena.

JASPER
This stone is usually striped, spotted, or multi-coloured – it is rarely all one colour. Boulders of jasper can weigh up to several hundred kilos.

JASPER SLAB

MYTH AND MAGIC
• In the Middle Ages, bloodstone was thought to hold drops of Christ's blood and to be all-powerful.
• In Renaissance times, sardonyx was worn by wives to bring about marital happiness.

Characteristic red spots and veins

BLOODSTONE
Polished slabs of bloodstone are often used decoratively as inlay or as cameos. The red spots in this stone are due to traces of iron oxides.

 Cabochon Bead   Cameo   Polished

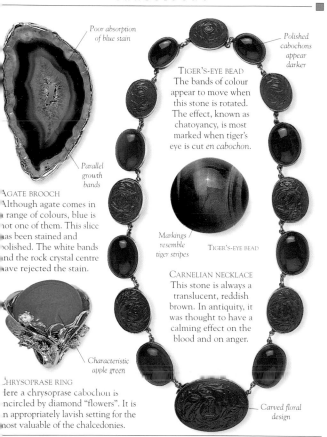

Poor absorption of blue stain

Polished cabochons appear darker

TIGER'S-EYE BEAD
The bands of colour appear to move when this stone is rotated. The effect, known as chatoyancy, is most marked when tiger's eye is cut en *cabochon*.

Parallel growth bands

AGATE BROOCH
Although agate comes in a range of colours, blue is not one of them. This slice has been stained and polished. The white bands and the rock crystal centre have rejected the stain.

Markings resemble tiger stripes

TIGER'S-EYE BEAD

CARNELIAN NECKLACE
This stone is always a translucent, reddish brown. In antiquity, it was thought to have a calming effect on the blood and on anger.

Characteristic apple green

CHRYSOPRASE RING
Here a chrysoprase cabochon is encircled by diamond "flowers". It is an appropriately lavish setting for the most valuable of the chalcedonies.

Carved floral design

JADE

TWO DISTINCT MINERALS, jadeite and nephrite, are recognized as jade. Nephrite is the more common and has been carved for thousands of years. Jadeite is slightly harder, often appears dimpled when polished, and comes in virtually every colour.

CARVED JADEITE
This Chinese pomander once contained aromatic substances. It is suspended from a tourmaline bead and string of seed pearls.

JADEITE
Black inclusions can be seen throughout this polished jadeite pebble. It is translucent with a greasy lustre.

MYTH AND MAGIC

• In China, children wore small jade amulets to prevent disease.

• Powdered and distilled in dew water, jade was believed to calm the mind.

• Its name comes from the Spanish *piedra de hijada*, loin stone, as jade was thought to cure hip problems.

Jadeit bead

IMPERIAL JAD
This unusuall
long string o
beads is of th
finest quality jadeit
known as imperia
jade, typified by its ric
emerald-green hue

Rich imperial green shade

Bead   Cameo   Polished

YELLOW JADE
Carved in the shape of a purse with drawstrings, this Chinese pomander is worked in fine, yellow-toned jadeite. Each side is decorated with an insect hovering over flowering sprigs.

Seven-character inscription

Even white colour

WHITE JADE
The base of this intricate box is carved in the shape of two peaches joined together on a leafy branch. Its white colour results from the absence of iron.

Box cover depicts descending crane

CHINESE CAMEL
Here the artist has used the shape of the stone for inspiration. With minimal carving, he has transformed the nephrite into a resting camel.

WHITE NEPHRITE CAMEL

JADEITE BANGLE
Jade is an extremely tough gemstone despite being only 7 on Mohs' scale of hardness. This is due to its structure – a mass of tiny interlocking grains and fibres.

ANTIQUE BEADS
The lilac colouring of this jadeite necklace is due to traces of manganese. Knots prevent the beads from damaging each other.

LILAC BEADS

PERIDOT

THE MOST IMPORTANT deposits of peridot are on the so-called "serpent isle" – the volcanic island of Zebirget in the Red Sea. According to Greek legend, vicious snakes lived on the island, guarding the precious stone and killing anyone who dared to approach it.

Step-cut drop

PERIDOTS AND DIAMONDS
Peridot's rich, oily green colour depends on its iron content. The stone is often cut as a pendeloque, as on the left, to create a darker, more favoured, hue.

OVAL MIXED CUT
Peridot has strong double refraction, which means that you can often see a doubling of the back facets.

MYTH AND MAGIC

• The early Egyptians claimed that peridot glowed by night but was invisible by day.

• In the Middle Ages, peridot was believed to dispel the darkness and terrors of the night.

• King Edward VII of England used to wear a peridot for good luck.

Intaglio design – carved inwards

CARVED SIGNET RING
This ring is probably of Roman origin and would have been commissioned by the gentleman featured. He would have used it to seal his letters.

| Step | Cabochon | Table | Cameo | Pendeloque |

HARDNESS 6.5

82

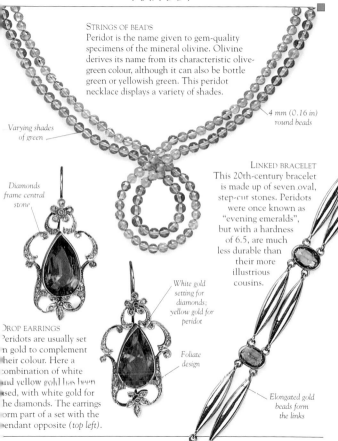

STRINGS OF BEADS
Peridot is the name given to gem-quality specimens of the mineral olivine. Olivine derives its name from its characteristic olive-green colour, although it can also be bottle green or yellowish green. This peridot necklace displays a variety of shades.

4 mm (0.16 in) round beads

Varying shades of green

LINKED BRACELET
This 20th-century bracelet is made up of seven oval, step-cut stones. Peridots were once known as "evening emeralds", but with a hardness of 6.5, are much less durable than their more illustrious cousins.

Diamonds frame central stone

White gold setting for diamonds; yellow gold for peridot

Foliate design

DROP EARRINGS
Peridots are usually set in gold to complement their colour. Here a combination of white and yellow gold has been used, with white gold for the diamonds. The earrings form part of a set with the pendant opposite (*top left*).

Elongated gold beads form the links

MOONSTONE

REMINISCENT OF the silvery moon, this stone derives its name from its blue-white sheen. Indeed it was once thought that the gem's lustre waxed and waned just like the moon itself, and moonstones have always been used in jewellery by moon-worshippers. In reality, the stone's distinctive sheen comes from its structure: thin albite layers create an attractive blue; thicker layers a more milky opalescence.

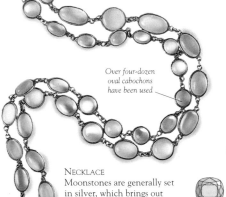

The stones have a bluish sheen

Over four-dozen oval cabochons have been used

CUSHION BRILLIANT CUT
The relative flatness of the cushion cut refracts the light in such a way as to enhance the opalescence of the stone

NECKLACE
Moonstones are generally set in silver, which brings out their characteristic bluish-silvery sheen.

Cushion   Cabochon   Cameo

HARDNESS 6–6.5

EASTERN EARRINGS
These earrings from Afghanistan show the moonstone's range of hues. The hanging drops are considerably lighter than the four upper ones.

The single drops are "moon-coloured"

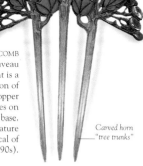

HORN COMB
This Art Nouveau hair-ornament is a combination of enamelled copper and moonstones on a carved horn base. Designs from nature were typical of the period (1890s).

Carved horn "tree trunks"

CUFFLINKS
Large cabochons form the sides of these cufflinks, designed by Carl Fabergé c.1910. The moonstones' pink sheen is due to the setting.

Gold setting lends a golden, pinkish tinge

Pattern carved into stone

TURTLE BROOCH
The distinctive markings of the turtle's upper shell are carved into the moonstone in this unusual piece (c.1900). The diamonds set in the legs and head are cushion cut.

MYTH AND MAGIC
• In India, the moonstone is believed to bring good luck and is considered sacred.

• The Romans thought that the wearers of moonstones would receive wisdom, wealth, and success in battle.

OPAL

UNLIKE OTHER GEMSTONES, the opal is non-crystalline and is formed from a hardened silica gel. It is known for its rainbow iridescence. The name opal is thought to be derived from the Sanskrit *upala*, meaning "precious stone". The opals used in ancient times came from the former Czechoslovakia, but today most are mined in Australia.

Large black opal

EDWARDIAN RING
Here the opal is cut *en cabochon* and reveals a milky-blue iridescence. The ring dates from the early 1900s.

SAMURAI PENDANT
Precious opal with a dark background, as in this unusual Art Deco pendant, is known as black opal. Here the "face" is dark, matching the stone below, while that on the other side is lighter.

MYTH AND MAGIC
• In Europe the opal is regarded as unlucky. Its reputation dates from the 14th century when many thought it had caused the plague known as the "Black Death".

• In Asia the stone is viewed more favourably. It is a symbol of hope.

UNMOUNTED BLACK OPAL
Despite displaying a predominance of light colours, this uncut stone is of precious black opal. It weighs more than 9 carats.

Silica structure disperses colour

Cameo

Step

Cabochon

HARDNESS 5.5–6.5

BROOCH
Milky opal
cabochons are
interspersed
with diamonds in this
classically elegant bar brooch.
The opals show flashes of pale
pinks, blues, and greens.

*Opal cabochons ranged
in decreasing size*

Fossilized shell

OPALIZED FOSSIL
Opal is found in
fossilized shell, wood,
and bone. In this shell, the
play of colour is caused by
the diffraction of light off its
closely packed silica spheres.

*Diamonds
frame the
large opals*

WINGS OF A BUTTERFLY
Victorian designs
paid homage to nature.
Moths, bumble-bees, and
dragonflies were especially
popular. Here four large
opals form the delicate
wings of a butterfly.

FIRE OPAL
Named for their deep orange
colour, most fire opals are
translucent or transparent.
They are extremely fragile
and suffer from changes
in temperature,
humidity, and
even light
intensity.

*Shimmering
bands of colour*

TURQUOISE

FIRST MINED OVER 6,000 years ago, turquoise has
a rich and colourful history. To the Aztecs it was
the "stone of the gods" and was used extensively
for religious artefacts; in medieval Europe it
was deemed a powerful talisman. Today most
commercial turquoise comes from China and
the southwestern states
of the United States.

CHILD'S NECKLACE

Turquoise forms in solid,
grape-like masses and as
nodules, often containing
dark veins, as can be seen
here. White enamelled
links join the stones in
this unusual Italian piece.

*Floral motif
engraved in
gold*

PERSIAN BLUE

Inlaid with gold leaf, this
good-luck charm is of the
finest sky-blue turquoise,
which is mined in Iran.
Its distinctive colour
comes from the presence
of copper. Traces of iron
cause a greenish tint.

MYTH AND MAGIC

• Turquoise has always
been considered lucky
and able to safeguard or
bring happiness.

• According to a
15th-century legend,
the stone loses its colour
when its owner is
unwell or in danger and
regains its brilliance
when the illness, or
danger, has passed.

Bead   Cabochon   Cameo

Carved
turquoise

RABBIT EARRINGS

In China, turquoise beads are often carved into a variety of animal shapes, as in these contemporary rabbit earrings. Here the silver "feathers" lend them a distinctly Native American flavour.

Hundreds of
cabochons
form the body

Vast turquoise
stone set in gold

MAMMOTH RING

The colour of turquoise is affected by heat, as well as by oils, cosmetics, and perspiration, and is liable to go from blue to a dull green. In order to avoid any risk of damage, it is best to remove turquoise rings before washing your hands.

SERPENT NECKLACE

The serpent was a favourite motif for necklaces in this Victorian times. When coiled around the base of the throat in a complete circle it symbolized eternal love.

LIZARD

Turquoise cabochons surround a spine of diamonds in this 19th-century brooch. The eyes are set with brilliant-cut rubies to make them stand out.

Tipped with 45
small turquoises

LAPIS LAZULI

PRIZED FOR ITS INTENSE BLUE colour, lapis lazuli has been used in jewellery, carvings, and amulets for thousands of years. Its name derives from medieval Latin and means "blue stone". The Egyptians regarded lapis as a heavenly stone and often used it on the statues of their gods and in burial masks as protection for the next life.

LUCKY HAND
This pendant is doubly powerful – the lapis offers protection against evil, and the clenched fist is a good-luck charm.

ROCK
Lapis is made up of several minerals, but its main ingredient is lazurite. The best quality lapis has a high proportion of lazurite.

White calcite

Dragon-head hook

CARVED LAPIS
This dragon garment hook is carved in high relief. The many tiny crystals in lapis make it an ideal material for carving.

IMITATION LAPIS
The French manufacturer Pierre Gilson created an artificial lapis using lazurite. The imitation stone has a similar composition to natural lapis, but is slightly softer.

Cabochon

Cameo

Polished

HARDNESS 5–5.5

TIFFANY NECKLACE
The American jeweller Tiffany
designed this fine lapis and
jade necklace. The beads are
carved, and every alternate
one is cupped in gold
filigree. The lapis
is of a rich, dark
blue variety.

Sulphur gives
rich blue colour

Single bead
of jade

Thickly
cut slices
of lapis

CONTEMPORARY EARRINGS
Lapis is hard enough to take a
good polish. These stones
come from the United States,
which is known for its dark,
high-quality lapis. Afghanistan
is another important source.

Intricately
carved surface

CARTIER BANGLE
Dating from the
1950s, this carved
bangle is the work
of the Parisian
design house
Cartier. The piece
is in the form of a
chimera – a mythical
fire-breathing monster.

Carved from
a single piece
of lapis

MYTH AND MAGIC

• Both the ancient
Egyptians and
Babylonians
believed that lapis
lazuli could cure
melancholy.

• Lapis lazuli is
used in Chinese
medicine to treat
phlegm, congestion,
and spasms.

AZURITE AND MALACHITE

THESE TWO STONES have a similar chemistry and history. Both are copper-based, both have been crushed and used as pigments, and both have been worked for thousands of years. The ancient Egyptians wore malachite as jewellery and used azurite for carving ornaments.

Azurite "donut"

AZURITE PENDANT

Azurite derives its name from its azure-blue colour. It is typically used for ornamental objects and simple jewellery, such as this circular pendant.

Band of azurite

POLISHED AZURITE
Azurite often intergrows with malachite, creating fabulous colour effects. Here, bands of green malachite can be seen with the distinctive bright blue azurite crystals.

Band of malachite

MYTH AND MAGIC

• During the Middle Ages, malachite was used as a cure for vomiting.

• Worn by children, malachite was thought to protect them and to keep evil spirits at bay.

• The ancient Egyptians used malachite amulets to ward off evil.

Characteristic azure blue

AZURITE

Cameo

Cabochon

ROCK OF AZURITE
Azurite occurs as short crystals or in spherical lumps as here. Copper gives the stone its distinctive colour.

HARDNESS 3.5–4

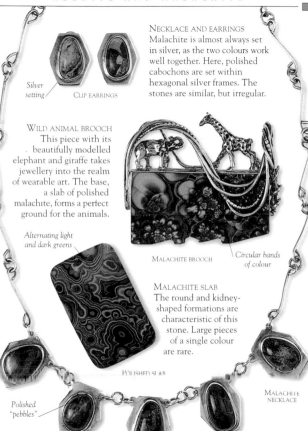

NECKLACE AND EARRINGS
Malachite is almost always set in silver, as the two colours work well together. Here, polished cabochons are set within hexagonal silver frames. The stones are similar, but irregular.

Silver setting

CLIP EARRINGS

WILD ANIMAL BROOCH
This piece with its beautifully modelled elephant and giraffe takes jewellery into the realm of wearable art. The base, a slab of polished malachite, forms a perfect ground for the animals.

Alternating light and dark greens

MALACHITE BROOCH

Circular bands of colour

MALACHITE SLAB
The round and kidney-shaped formations are characteristic of this stone. Large pieces of a single colour are rare.

POLISHED SLAB

MALACHITE NECKLACE

Polished "pebbles"

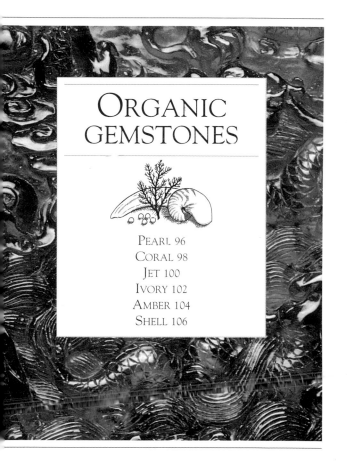

ORGANIC
GEMSTONES

PEARL

ONCE VIEWED BY ARABIANS as tears of the gods, pearls are created by certain shellfish, mainly oysters and mussels. They form when an irritant such as a grain of sand enters the shell. The mollusc then secretes layer upon layer of calcium carbonate, known as "nacre", around the foreign body. It is this innate defence mechanism that creates the bead of pearl.

NATURAL PEARL IN OYSTER SHELL
The term "natural pearl" refers to a pearl which has formed as an accident of nature and not by human intervention. Such pearls are rare and valuable.

The pearl is still attached to the shell lining

SEED PEARL BRACELET
Pearls vary in size from a millimetre in diameter to as large as a pigeon's egg! Their weight is given in grains, 1 grain = .05 g (0.002 oz). Seed pearls weigh less than 0.25 grain.

Perfect size, form, and colour

CULTURED PEARLS
It is virtually impossible to find natural pearls that match. This string is of cultured pearls, produced artificially by inserting beads of clam shell into oysters.

Strings of cultured seed pearls

Bead

So-called black pearls are gun-metal coloured

Triton, son of Poseidon, Greek god of the seas

Small baroque pearl

Natural pearls take up to seven years to form

GRAPE EARRINGS
The multicoloured pearls in these early 20th-century earrings are probably produced by Tahitian Black Lip oysters. These oysters secrete a dark pigment directly into the pearly strata.

Cultured pearls take up to four years to form

CANNING JEWEL
Irregularly shaped pearls are known as baroque pearls. The 16th-century Triton, above, has four, with the largest one forming the body. It is fitting that a sea god is made up of pearls – the "fruits" of the sea.

Classic cream-white colour

MYTH AND MAGIC

• According to the Roman writer Pliny, Cleopatra dissolved a priceless pearl earring in her wine and drank it as a testament of love for Antony.

• Pearls have long been used medicinally. They were thought to cure everything from fevers to stomach ulcers.

CORAL

MOST CORAL, namely red, pink, white, and blue varieties, consists of a substance similar to that of pearls – calcium carbonate – but that is where the similarity ends. Coral is formed by the build up of skeletal remains of colonies of tiny marine animals known as coral polyps. It grows in branchlike formations.

Hand of good luck

RED CORAL
This sprig of red coral comes from the warm waters of the Mediterranean. It has a distinctive "wood-grain" pattern on the surface of its branches.

Branch-like structure

CHILD'S BRACELET
Coral was thought to protect the wearer against evil; children in particular were given coral jewellery to ensure their safety and keep them healthy.

CORAL FRAGMENT NECKLACE
Large pieces of coral are relatively rare and so are saved for decorative objects or cameos. Branches too small for beads may be fashioned into "sprig" strings.

POLISHED CABOCHON
Coral has been used in jewellery for thousands of years. The deeper the colour, the more prized the coral is.

Bead

Cabochon

Cameo

HARDNESS 3

Highly polished cabochon

BLACK CORAL
Black and golden corals differ structurally from other varieties. They are composed of an organic, hornlike substance called conchiolin.

AFRICAN NECKLACE
Unworked coral has a dull, horny appearance. To become "gem" quality, the outer crust has to be removed. The coral is then cut, usually with a saw or knife, shaped as desired, and polished.

Hundreds of rough corals

WHITE CORAL BROOCH
A large oval cabochon is framed by diamonds and ten white coral beads in this gold-mounted brooch. In the early 1900s, it was fashionable to marry the humble coral with the world's rarest and most precious gemstone.

PALE PINK
Graduated cabochons of the palest pink are interspersed with diamonds in this ring, which dates from about 1900. It was probably given as a 35th-wedding anniversary present.

Monkey on a blossom tree

MONKEY CARVING
The relative softness of coral means that it is quite easy to carve. This piece is of Eastern origin; much pink coral is taken from the waters around Japan.

MYTH AND MAGIC
• In the 16th century, people thought that a sprig of red or white coral could calm a raging tempest.

• Coral allegedly cured madness and protected against enchantments.

JET

A PRODUCT OF FOSSILIZED WOOD, jet is similar to coal, only harder and more durable. Jet forms when the remains of wood are immersed in stagnant water for hundreds of years and then buried and compacted under intense pressure. In the 19th century, jet became popular for mourning jewellery, because of its colour. Glass, onyx, and a type of rubber known as vulcanite, are used as imitation jet.

Whitby jet

JET BRACELET
Faceted, flat, oval plates of jet are strung together in this polished 19th century bangle.

SYMBOLIC BROOCH
The dove symbolizes peace and salvation. Here it is coupled with a heart, an emblem of love, in this finely carved remembrance brooch.

Carved jet

BLACK ROSE
Jet from Whitby, Yorkshire, is considered the best quality, because it takes such a good polish. This piece dates from the late 19th century and features a rose. It would have been worn by a woman in mourning.

DOVE OF PEACE

Polished   Bead   Cameo

HARDNESS 2.5

BEADED CLOTH
This delicate trim from a Victorian overskirt has beads of faceted jet sewn into the fabric, as was the fashion of the day. The beads create a gem-studded form of black lace, the scallop design edged by rows of black sequins.

ACORNS
Queen Victoria of England popularized jet by wearing it after the death of her husband, Prince Albert. Death was viewed as a passage into another life, and this acorn (which forms part of a necklace) reflects that sense of hope and renewal.

Trim of drilled jet beads

HAIR COMB
At its height of fashion, Whitby jet was exported all over Europe. Combs were popular in Spain, where they were used to hold up a lady's black mantilla – a lace veil worn in church.

Jet hair comb

MYTH AND MAGIC

• According to the Roman writer Pliny, jet mixed with the marrow of a stag could heal a serpent's bite.

• Powdered and mixed with beeswax, jet was used to reduce tumours, and mixed with wine, to alleviate toothache.

• In China, jet is seen as a symbol of winter.

IVORY

THE TERM "IVORY" is generally associated with elephant tusks, although it also includes the teeth or tusks of mammals such as the hippopotamus, boar, sea lion, and sperm whale. People have collected ivory for thousands of years, prizing it for its rich creamy colour and fine texture. It has always been a popular material for jewellery, ornaments, and amulets.

String of graduated beads

AFRICAN NECKLACE
The most highly prized ivory comes from Africa. It has a warm tint, is harder than its Indian equivalent, and shows very little grain.

Stylized crocodile

BROOCH
This 20th-century brooch was carved on the shores of Lake Malawi, an area known for crocodiles. As in many other parts of the world, Malawi has strict restrictions on the sale of ivory.

PATCHWORK BOX
Ivory is quite a soft material to work with and, because of its porous nature, can be dyed easily. Here slices of natural and stained ivory create a decorative surface for this small box.

INLAID BOX

Bead   Cameo   Polished

HARDNESS 2.5

POLISHED SECTION OF ELEPHANT TOOTH
This striated ivory slice is from the molar tooth of an elephant rather than the tusk. Its distinctive, curved lines show the growth pattern, and the many small vertical cracks are evidence of its age.

Growth lines

MOLAR TOOTH

• Acquiring an elephant's tusks was once thought to confer superhuman powers – to conquer such a mighty opponent was to be invincible.

• A symbol of purity, ivory was much used for making crucifixes.

Ivory face with ruby eyes

DEVIL STICK PIN
Dating from around 1840, this ivory hat pin is carved in the form of Lucifer's face, complete with gold horns and piercing ruby eyes. Like the more common carved skull, it is a *memento mori* – a playful reminder of human mortality.

Uniformly carved beads

CARVED BEADS
The carved beads here have a distinctly organic feel, resembling a rare tropical fruit. The necklace is of African origin, although India, Myanmar (Burma), and Indonesia are also significant sources of elephant ivory.

AMBER

FORMED FROM THE fossilized resin of trees that lived millions of years ago, amber has been used for jewellery and religious objects since prehistoric times. It was believed to have talismanic properties, and many ancient peoples buried amber objects and amulets with their dead to protect them in the afterlife. It is usually a golden orange colour.

Insects trapped within the resin

PENDANT
Plants and insects may become trapped within the sticky resin before it sets. In this extraordinary pendant from London's Natural History Museum, a spider and a cricket are visible.

Rough pebble found washed up on beach

BALTIC AMBER
Most commercial amber comes from the Baltic coasts of Poland and the former USSR, although other notable deposits are in Sicily and Myanmar (Burma). Amber tends to be found in soft sediments or in the sea. It is occasionally washed ashore after heavy storms have dislodged it from the sea bed.

GOLDEN BEADS
These honey-toned, antique beads are of an opaque variety and have aged well. Amber has a tendency to dry out and crack if left in the sun or worn in the heat of the day.

| Bead | Cabochon | Cameo | Polished |

HARDNESS 2.5

DANISH AMBER

This fossilized pebble is a mixture of clear and cloudy amber and was found along the Danish coast. Amber is not as dense as synthetic and plastic resins and will float in salt water.

Cloudy, opaque areas

DARK RED BEADS

The rich red tones of this necklace suggest that the amber originated in China; Baltic examples tend to be pale yellow or golden. Here over fifty drilled, faceted, and polished beads have been used.

Chinese amber

ELECTRIC CHARGE

This translucent bead has a resinous lustre and hints of cracks. Amber is known for producing an electrical charge when rubbed. It is from the Greek name for amber, *elektron*, that the word electricity is derived.

GOLDEN GRAPES

Amber's relative softness makes it easy to carve, as can be seen in the glistening grapes, which dangle from the overhanging leaf. This brooch is of Baltic origin.

DROP EARRINGS

These amber and gold earrings are of Italian design. The air bubbles and inclusions give amber its characteristic mottled appearance and are not seen as flaws. However, this opaqueness can be removed by boiling the fossil resin in oil.

MYTH AND MAGIC

• Sacred to the Greek sun god Apollo, amber was once thought to be congealed sunlight.

• Amber was also viewed as tears for the Vikings, Freya's tears for Svipdag, and for the ancient Greeks, tears over the death of Phaeton.

SHELL

THESE OFFERINGS from the sea have been used as items of adornment for thousands of years. Conch shells, with their pink and white layers, have been fashioned into cameos since Roman times, and the use of mother-of-pearl, the iridescent lining of many shells, goes back still further. Tortoiseshell, the hard shell of the hawksbill turtle, has been made into countless boxes, bangles, and hair ornaments over the years.

CAMEO
This cameo dates from c.1900. It was common then for cameos to reflect classical scenes, paying homage to ancient empires

TIGER COWRIE CAMEO
To create a cameo, layers of shell are carved away to reveal the different colours. It takes great skill to create a realistic image.

HAIR COMB
At one time, tortoiseshell was the most popular material for hair ornaments, such as this comb. Today, because of over-fishing, most are made out of plastic.

Mottled colours

TIGER COWRIE SHELL

Cabochon   Cameo   Polished

HARDNESS 2.5

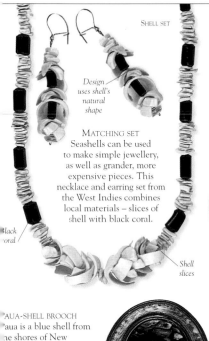

SHELL SET

Design uses shell's natural shape

MATCHING SET
Seashells can be used to make simple jewellery, as well as grander, more expensive pieces. This necklace and earring set from the West Indies combines local materials – slices of shell with black coral.

Black coral

Shell slices

TREASURE BOX
Here, a silver lid and clasp have transformed this shell into a box. The shell is of the "turban" family and comes from the Indian Ocean; the green tones are not natural but the result of a dye.

Dyed shell

Silver lid

PAUA-SHELL BROOCH
Paua is a blue shell from the shores of New Zealand. It is part of the abalone family, but characteristically has far richer tones of blues, greens, and purples. Here a cabochon from the mother-of-pearl lining has been framed in copper and silver.

MYTH AND MAGIC
• In China, mother-of-pearl has been prescribed for over 1,000 years. It is used for heart palpitations, dizziness, and high blood pressure

• Venus, goddess of love, is believed to have emerged from the sea in a giant scallop shell.

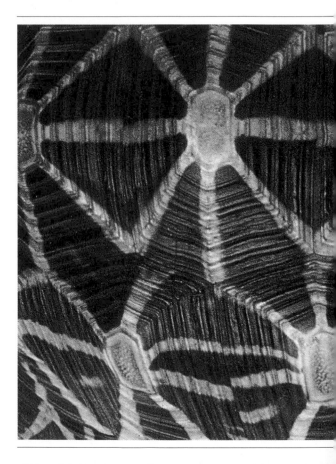

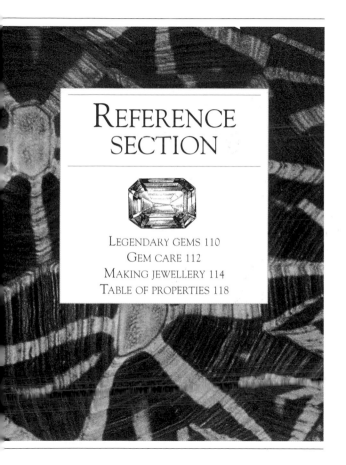

REFERENCE
SECTION

LEGENDARY GEMS

IT IS NO WONDER that there are so many stories surrounding gemstones. They represent money and glamour, desired by all, but owned by few. Precious stones have been the cause of countless thefts, strange events, and even murders, some of which are recounted here.

THE BOLDNESS OF CAPTAIN BLOOD

During the reign of Charles II of England (1660–85), Blood, a former army officer, attempted to steal the crown jewels from the Tower of London. Disguised as a parson, he befriended the Master of the Jewel-House. Then one day he and his friends bludgeoned the 80-year-old warder with a mallet and seized the royal regalia. However, the burglary was interrupted by the arrival of the warder's son, who raised the alarm. The thieves headed for the wharf with their booty, dropping the sceptre in their haste, but were overtaken, and the crown, globe, and sceptre were returned to their rightful place.

TOWER OF LONDON

MISTAKEN IDENTITY

In 1740 a gigantic diamond was found in Brazil, valued at millions of pounds. The stone became the prized property of the Braganza's, the Portuguese royal family, and then disappeared from view. It is believed to have been set in the Portuguese crown jewels. If this is the case, then the famous Braganza Diamond is in fact only a humble, albeit beautiful, aquamarine.

MODEL OF THE BRAGANZA

THE CAT'S-EYE CATASTROPHE

The French queen Marie Antoinette gave a massive cat's-eye ring to a devoted admirer of hers – the Swedish Count Axel de Fersen. After her death during the French Revolution, Count Fersen never removed the ring from his left hand, and he was wearing it when he was stoned to death on the steps of Stockholm Cathedral some years later. One of his attackers allegedly hacked

his finger off with an axe, and threw the ring, finger and all, into the sea. But the ring returned to haunt the man, who imagined he was being threatened by a disembodied hand.

MARIE-ANTOINETTE

A JINXED JEWEL

King Alfonso XII of Spain jilted his fiancée, the countess of Castiglione, in favour of a princess of royal blood. The Countess sent her betrayer a wedding present of a superb opal, knowing it to be a stone of ill-omen. Within months, Alfonso's new bride was dead. The King then gave the ring to his grandmother, and she, too, died. His sister soon followed, and finally King Alfonso himself fell victim to the opal's curse.

MYSTERY THEFT

On October 14, 1946, the Duchess of Windsor (wife of the former English king Edward VIII) had her jewel

DUKE AND DUCHESS OF WINDSOR

case stolen from her stately home in Ednam, England. Strangely, the duchess' dog didn't bark, the jewels were under her maid's bed rather than safely under lock and key, and none of the stated contents of the case were ever recovered. Nevertheless, the insurers paid the full amount of the claim – about £24,000 – and the delighted duchess was able to buy the first of her Cartier panther jewels, a brooch of a big cat on a magnificent 90-carat emerald cushion

CARTIER PANTHER

SMASH AND GRAB

In August 1958, the illustrious New York jeweller Tiffany & Co was the victim of a daring robbery. Early one Sunday morning, two men leaped out of a car and smashed the store windows. In just minutes they grabbed thousands of pounds worth of diamonds. The jewels were never recovered.

LIPPERT'S LUGGAGE

In September 1989, Felice Lippert, co-founder of Weight Watchers International, mysteriously lost her handbag containing half-a-million dollars of uninsured jewellery. At Miami's Palm Beach airport, she placed her bag on the X-ray machine's conveyor belt and the bag disappeared, never to be seen again!

GEM CARE

GEMSTONES HAVE LASTED for millions of years underground. However, once mined and made into jewellery, they are exposed to conditions and chemicals that can affect their life spans. Precious stones may fracture, break, lose their shine, or even change colour if they are not cared for properly.

STORAGE OF GEMSTONES

Store each piece separately, as harder gemstones, such as diamonds and rubies, will scratch softer ones. Particular care should be taken with the organics, as they are all extremely soft and liable to damage. Jewellery should be kept in individual boxes, in compartments in a jewellery box, or wrapped in cloth or tissue paper.

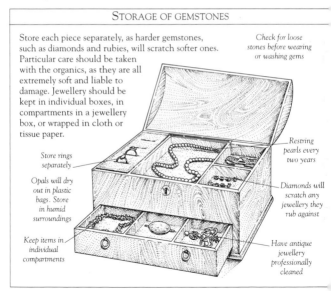

Check for loose stones before wearing or washing gems

Store rings separately

Opals will dry out in plastic bags. Store in humid surroundings

Keep items in individual compartments

Restring pearls every two years

Diamonds will scratch any jewellery they rub against

Have antique jewellery professionally cleaned

CARE AND CLEANING OF GEMSTONES

Remove jewellery before doing any gardening or housework. Clean gems regularly using warm water and bar soap, or a dilute vinegar solution, unless specific instructions are given below. Washing-up liquid is too harsh to use on organic gems. It should also be avoided with emeralds and rubies, since it will strip them of any oil that may have been applied. Never wear organic gems in swimming pools.

SOAP

SOFT CLOTH

TOOTHBRUSH

WASHING -UP LIQUID

BOWL

ORGANIC GEMSTONES	
Pearl	Pearls are damaged by perfume, hairspray, detergents, and perspiration. Apply perfumes or cosmetics before putting pearls on. Wipe with a damp cloth after wearing.
Coral	Perspiration will affect coral, dulling the colour. Avoid all chemicals. Never soak. To clean, use a damp cloth.
Amber and ivory	Avoid contact with hairspray, perfumes, and cosmetics. To clean, wash in warm water with soap and wipe dry.
MINERAL GEMSTONES	
Diamond	Diamonds attract grease. Clean with a toothbrush in warm water and soap or washing-up liquid, or in alcohol.
Opal	Opals may crack in freezing conditions and lose colour in excessive heat. Never wash in hot water.
Turquoise	Liable to crack in extremes of temperature. Avoid contact with perfumes and cosmetics, which may cause stones to turn green. To clean, wipe with a damp cloth. Never soak.

MAKING JEWELLERY

USE THE FOLLOWING step-by-step guide to make a pair of earrings and matching necklace. We have used multicoloured tourmalines in this example, but you can substitute any stones of a similar size. If you are using gemstones of different colours, plan your pattern before you start in order to be certain that you have enough of each colour.

TOURMALINE EARRINGS

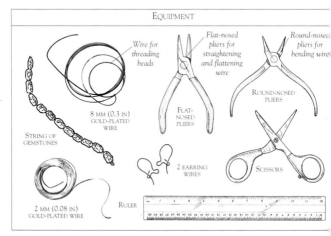

EQUIPMENT

Wire for threading beads

8 MM (0.3 IN) GOLD-PLATED WIRE

Flat-nosed pliers for straightening and flattening wire

FLAT-NOSED PLIERS

Round-nosed pliers for bending wire

ROUND-NOSED PLIERS

STRING OF GEMSTONES

2 EARRING WIRES

SCISSORS

2 MM (0.08 IN) GOLD-PLATED WIRE

RULER

EARRINGS

1

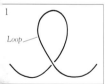

Loop

1 Cut a 6-cm (2.3-in) length of thick wire and bend it to form a loop.

2

Leave ends open

2 Make two small loops, leaving ends slightly open.

3

Tight flat coil

3 Cut three 5-cm (2-in) lengths of thin wire. Make tight flat coil at one end of piece of the thin wire and thread stone onto it.

4

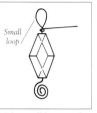

Small loop

4 Make small loop at other end and twist wire over itself to secure.

5

New loop

5 Trim excess wire to avoid sharp edges. Thread a new piece of thin wire through existing loop and loop and twist wire again.

6 Thread another gemstone onto this wire, make loop, and carry on as before. Repeat steps 5 and 6 to make "V" shape.

6

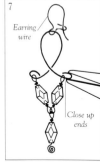

"V" shape

Detail of links

7

Earring wire

Close up ends

7 Secure the two stones onto the thick wire and close up end loops with pliers. Place completed earring onto earring wire. Repeat whole process for second earring.

NECKLACE

1 Cut six 6-cm (2.3-in) lengths and twenty 3-cm (1.2-in) lengths of thick wire. Cut twelve 5-cm (2-in) lengths of thin wire.

2 Bend one 6-cm strand of thick wire as per earrings stages 1 and 2.

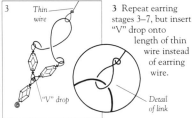

Thin wire

"V" drop

Detail of link

3 Repeat earring stages 3–7, but insert "V" drop onto length of thin wire instead of earring wire.

Thread gem onto thin wire

4 Loop and secure thin wire as before and thread gemstone onto it. Put to one side to use in stage 7.

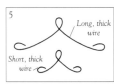

Long, thick wire

Short, thick wire

5 Bend four short, and five long, thick wires at centre to form small loops and curl up ends.

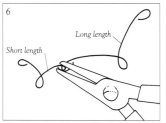

Short length

Long length

6 Link together the loops at the end of each short and long piece. Secure by closing the loops with pliers.

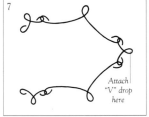

Attach "V" drop here

7 The long and short lengths should make an alternating pattern. Attach "V" drop to central link.

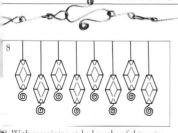

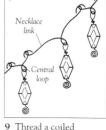

9

Necklace link

Central loop

8

8 With remaining eight lengths of thin wire, make coils as per earring stage 2 and thread a gemstone onto each strand.

9 Thread a coiled gemstone drop through the central loop of each necklace link. Secure as before and trim off any excess wire.

10

"S" shape   *Figure-of-eight*

10 Bend eight 3-cm (1.2-in) lengths of thick wire into figure-of-eights and eight into elongated "S" shapes.

11

Figure-of-eight link

"S"-shape link

11 Join lengths together to make alternating pattern. Attach eight links to each side of necklace.

CLASP

1 Cut one 11-cm (4.3-in) and one 3 cm (1.2 in) length of thick wire.

Secure "V" drop to centre of main necklace

2

2 Coil and bend longer wire into figure-of-eight. Attach to necklace.

3

Clasp

Oval loop

3 Thread shorter wire onto other end of necklace and form oval loop large enough to hook clasp into it.

TABLE OF PROPERTIES

THIS TABLE SETS OUT the main features of each type of gem along with a rough guide as to its value. The gemstones are divided into eight categories, depending on their crystal structures (see page 22). Hardness is measured according to Mohs' scale, which classifies minerals relative to each other on a scale of 1 to 10 (see page 24). The gemstones' specific gravity (SG) is their weight compared with the weight of an equal volume of water (see page 24). The value of each gem is calculated on the basis of an 8-mm (0.3-in) diameter, cabochon-cut stone of average quality. Where cabochon cuts do not apply, prices for faceted gems are given.

The price guide is as follows: £ = under £5; ££ = £5–£10; £££ = £10–£20; ££££ = over £20.

NAME	STRUCTURE	HARDNESS	SG	PRICE
Achroite (Tourmaline)	Trigonal	7.5	3.06	£££
Agate (Chalcedony)	Amorphous	7	2.61	£
Almandine (Garnet)	Cubic	7.5	4.00	£
Amber	Amorphous	2.5	1.08	£
Amethyst (Quartz)	Trigonal	7	2.65	£
Aquamarine (Beryl)	Hexagonal	7.5	2.69	£££
Azurite	Monoclinic	3.5	3.77	£
Bloodstone (Chalcedony)	Amorphous	7	2.61	£
Carnelian (Chalcedony)	Amorphous	7	2.61	£
Chalcedony	Amorphous	7	2.61	£
Chatoyant Quartz	Trigonal	7	2.65	£
Chrysoberyl	Orthorhombic	8.5	3.71	££££

Name	Structure	Hardness	SG	Price
Chrysoprase (Chalcedony)	Amorphous	7	2.61	£
Citrine (Quartz)	Trigonal	7	2.65	£
Coral	Amorphous	3	2.68	£
Demantoid (Garnet)	Cubic	6.5	3.85	£ £
Diamond	Cubic	10	3.52	£ £ £ £
Dravite (Tourmaline)	Trigonal	7.5	3.06	£ £
Emerald (Beryl)	Hexagonal	7.5	2.71	£ £ £ £
Fire Agate (Chalcedony)	Amorphous	7	2.61	£ £
Grossular (Garnet)	Cubic	7	3.49	£
Hauyne	Cubic	6	2.40	£ £
Hessonite (Grossular Garnet)	Cubic	7.25	3.65	£
Ivory	Amorphous	2.5	1.90	N/A
Jadeite (Jade)	Amorphous	7	3.33	£
Jasper (Chalcedony)	Amorphous	7	2.61	£
Jet	Amorphous	2.5	1.33	£
Lapis Lazuli	Amorphous	5.5	2.80	£
Malachite	Monoclinic	4	3.80	£
Milky Quartz	Trigonal	7	2.65	£
Moonstone (Orthoclase)	Monoclinic	6	2.57	£
Nephrite (Jade)	Amorphous	6.5	2.96	£
Opal	Amorphous	6	2.10	£ £
Orthoclase	Monoclinic	6	2.56	£
Padparadscha (Corundum)	Trigonal	9	4.00	£ £ £ £
Pearl	Amorphous	3	2.71	£ £ £ £ *
Peridot	Orthorhombic	6.5	3.34	£ £ £
Pyrope (Garnet)	Cubic	7.25	3.80	£
Rock Crystal (Quartz)	Trigonal	7	2.65	£
Rose Quartz	Trigonal	7	2.65	£
Rubellite (Tourmaline)	Trigonal	7.5	3.06	£ £ £
Ruby (Corundum)	Trigonal	9	4.00	£ £ £ £
Sapphire (Corundum)	Trigonal	9	4.00	£ £ £ £
Sardonyx (Chalcedony)	Amorphous	7	2.61	£
Schorl (Tourmaline)	Trigonal	7.5	3.06	£ £
Shell	Amorphous	2.5	1.30	£
Spessartine (Garnet)	Cubic	7	4.16	£ £ £
Spinel	Cubic	8	3.60	£ £ £
Topaz	Orthorhombic	8	3.54	£ £
Turquoise	Amorphous	6	2.80	£
Uvarovite (Garnet)	Cubic	7.5	3.77	£ £ £ £
Watermelon Tourmaline	Trigonal	7.5	3.06	£ £
Zircon	Tetragonal	7.5	4.69	£ £

(*price given is for 8-mm [0.3-in] cultured pearls)

Glossary

ALBITE
Important variety of feldspar; occurs in many types of rock.

ALLUVIAL DEPOSITS
Concentrations of material that have been separated by weathering from the host rock, then deposited by rivers and streams.

ALUMINOUS SHALE
Shale is a rock made of clay that has been buried and compacted. Aluminous shale contains traces of aluminium.

AMORPHOUS
Without regular internal atomic structure or external shape.

AMULET
Protective charm worn to ward off evil or illness, or to bring about good fortune.

ART DECO
Decorative style originating in Paris in the 1920s, marked by geometric motifs and well-defined outlines.

ART NOUVEAU
Late 19th-century style of art and architecture characterized by curved outlines often derived from nature.

BAGUETTE CUT
Rectangular step cut.

BASALT
Basalt rock forms at the earth's surface and cools rapidly. It consists of small, poorly developed crystals.

BRILLIANT CUT
Most popular cut for diamonds and many other stones, especially colourless ones. It ensures the maximum amount of light is reflected from the stone.

CABOCHON
A type of cut in which a gemstone has a domed upper surface.

CAMEO
Design in low relief, usually on a shell or type of agate, around which the background has been cut away.

CARAT
Standard measure of weight for precious stones. One carat equals 0.2 gram. The term is also used to describe the purity of gold. Pure gold is 24 carat.

CHATOYANCY
Cat's-eye effect shown by some stones when cut *en cabochon*. Light is reflected along thin, iridescent bands.

CLEAVAGE
The way a mineral breaks along certain planes according to its internal structure.

CROWN
Top section of a cut stone, above the girdle.

CRYSTALLINE
Having a crystal structure.

CRYSTAL STRUCTURE
Internal atomic structure of crystals. Crystalline gems are classified according to seven basic structures.

DICHROIC
Gem that appears to be two different colours or shades when viewed from different directions.

DIFFRACTION
The splitting of white light into its constituent colours.

DOUBLET
Composite stone made of two pieces cemented or glued together.

EROSION
The transportation of material from its original site by weathering, i.e. processes involving wind, water, and ice.

FACET
One surface of a cut gemstone.

FACETING
The cutting and polishing of the surfaces of a gemstone into facets. The style of cut is dependent on the number and shape of the facets.

FANCIES
Diamonds of an unusual natural colour.

FANCY CUT
Name given to a stone with an unconventional shape when cut.

FIRE
Term used for dispersed light. A gem with strong fire is unusually bright.

GIRDLE
Band around the widest part of a cut stone, where the crown meets the pavilion.

GRANITE
Coarse-grained igneous rock.

HEAT TREATMENT
Application of heat to a gem aimed at enhancing its colour or clarity.

IGNEOUS ROCK
Rock that has formed from erupted volcanic lava or solidified magma.

INCLUSIONS
Solid, liquid, or gaseous particles contained within a mineral. Often add interest to a stone.

INTAGLIO
Design in which the subject is cut lower than the background. Often used for signet rings.

INTERGROWN
When two or more minerals grow together and become interlocked.

IRIDESCENCE
Reflection of light caused by internal features of a gem, giving rise to a rainbow-like play of colours.

LAVA
Molten rock, erupted from volcanoes.

LUSTRE
The intensity of light reflected off a gem's surface.

MAGMA
Rock in a molten state below the Earth's surface.

MANTLE
Layer of the Earth between the core and the crust. It is about 2,900 km (1,740 miles) thick.

MATRIX
The rock in which a gem is found.

METAMORPHIC ROCK
Type of rock that forms from other rocks owing to the action of heat and pressure, or heat alone.

MICROCRYSTALLINE
Mineral structure in which crystals are too small to be seen with the naked eye.

MIXED CUT
Cut in which the facets above and below the girdle are styled in different ways, usually brilliant cut above and step cut below.

MOHS' SCALE
Measure of a mineral's hardness in relation to other minerals, on a scale of 1 to 10.

OILING
Process of applying mineral oil to certain stones, mainly emeralds, to mask their inclusions; turn the stones a darker, more favourable hue; and make them more transparent.

OPALESCENCE
Milky blue form of iridescence.

OPAQUE
Substance that does not allow light to pass through it.

PAVILION
Lower part of stone, below the girdle.

PEGMATITE
Igneous rock, which forms as the liquids from magma cool. It consists of unusually large crystals.

PENDELOQUE CUT
Lozenge-shaped, fancy cut, often used for flawed gems.

POROUS
Containing pores, or holes, that allow a substance to be penetrated by water, other fluids, or air.

RESIN
Sticky substance obtained from certain plants.

RIVER GRAVELS
Deposits of minerals that have been broken down and washed downstream, occasionally containing gemstones.

ROUGH
Term used to describe a rock or crystal still in its natural state, before cutting or polishing.

SEDIMENTARY ROCK
Type of rock at the Earth's surface. It consists of layers of rock fragments or other substances that have been deposited on top of each other and have hardened.

SILICA
Hard, glossy mineral usually occurring as quartz. Silica is the main constituent of sandstone.

SPECIFIC GRAVITY
The comparison of a mineral's weight with the weight of an equal volume of water.

SPECTROSCOPE
Instrument used to identify different gemstones. It reveals the bands of light

that a gemstone absorbs.

STEP CUT
Rectangular- or square-shaped cut with several facets parallel to the edges of the stone. It is generally used for coloured stones.

STRIATIONS
Parallel scratches, grooves or lines in a mineral.

SYNTHETIC GEMSTONE
Laboratory-made stone whose chemical composition and optical properties are similar to those of its natural equivalent.

TALISMAN
Good-luck charm believed to possess magical powers

TRANSLUCENT
Material that allows some light to pass through it.

TRANSPARENT
Material that allows light to pass through it.

VITREOUS
Glass-like quality (used to describe a gem's lustre).

WEATHERING
The breaking down of rocks by the action of various processes, such as freezing, thawing, and dissolving in water.

Resources

Amateur Geological Society
5 Village Road,
Finchley,
London N3 1TL

British Lapidary and Mineral Dealers Association (BLMDA)
7 Chapel Lane,
Stoke-on-Trent
ST7 3SD

Federation of Lapidary and Geological Societies
For directory of clubs and societies:
2a Allingham Court,
Haverstock Hill,
London NW3 2AH

Gemmological Association of Great Britain
27 Greville Street
London EC1N 8SU

Gem-Rock Museum
Chain Road, Creetown,
Kirkcudbrightshire
DG8 7HJ
The museum has many examples of cut gemstones and carvings and contains a lapidary workshop.

Natural History Museum
Cromwell Road,
South Kensington,
London SW7 5BD
The Earth Science Department contains an extensive collection of gemstones, rocks, and minerals.

Royal Museum of Scotland
Chambers Street,
Edinburgh EH1 1JF
Its collection of minerals are of international importance.

Scottish Mineral and Lapidary Club
22b St Giles Street,
Edinburgh EH1 1PT

Shell Museum
Glandford, near Holt,
Norfolk NR25 7JR
Houses a collection of shells from around the world, jewels, pottery, and agate ware.

Sidcup Lapidary and Mineral Society
16 Preston Drive,

Bexley Heath,
Kent DA7 4VQ

The Bead Shop
43 Neal Street,
London WC2H 9PJ
For catalogue and mail order:
JRM Beads Ltd,
16 Redbridge Ent. Centre,
Thompson Close,
Ilford,
Essex IG1 1TY

The Hunterian Museum
University of Glasgow,
University Avenue,
Glasgow
G12 8QQ
Exhibits a wide variety of gemstones and minerals.

UK Facet Cutters' Guild
54 Close Lane,
Alsager,
Stoke-on-Trent
ST7 2JT

Wessex Lapidary and Mineralogical Society
31 Abbots Way
Highfield,
Southampton,
Hampshire SO2 1NW

Index

Acknowledgements

Dorling Kindersley would like to thank:
Stephen Bradshaw of the jeweller Pearl Cross
Ltd for the generous loan of his jewellery;
Emma Foa for her handmade jewellery; Carole
Oliver for the loan of her personal jewellery;
Dennis Durham, gem cutter, for his expert
knowledge and patience; Fiona Gamble of the
jeweller Bentley & Co. for her unstinting
enthusiasm; David Mayor for his research into
traditional medicine; Hilary Bird for the index;
Tanya Tween, Robin Hunter, Earl Neish, and
Jacqui Burton, for design assistance; Caroline
Potts for picture library services.

Photographs by:
Steve Gorton. Additional photography by
Colin Keates, Harry Taylor, Mathew Ward.

Illustrations by:
Sarah Ponder, Aziz Khan, Janet Allis, John
Hutchinson, Peter Visscher, Caroline Church,
Janos Marffy, Alistair Wardle.

Picture Credits:
c=centre; b=bottom; l=left; r=right; t=top
The publisher would like to thank the
following for their kind permission to
reproduce their photographs:
**The Ancient Art and Architecture Collection
Ltd:** 14tr; **Amber Centre:** 105bl; **Courtesy of
Argos:** 69tr; **Bentley and Co:** 4c, 4cr, 5cl, 5cr,
7tc, 17bl, 50bc, 50br, 51crb, 54cl, 55cl, 57cla,
59cr, 62tr, 63cr, 64cla, 64bc, 65tr, 66tl, 67crb,
67cbl, 72cla, 73cl, 73br, 85bc, 86clb, 87br,
88–89, 89bc, 98cr;
Bridgeman Art Library: Cheltenham Art
Gallery and Museums, Gloucester: Hair comb
by Fred Partridge 85tr; Christie's Images 60cl;
Giraudon 12bl; Private Collection 101bl;
Bruce Coleman Ltd: Gerald Cubitt 18cl; Charles
and Sandra Hood 19cb; John Murray 32crb;
Christie's Images: 3c, 35br, 51t, 51br, 59bl,
62bc, 70bl, 71bl, 74clb, 76tl, 77tr, 77bl, 78cla,
80tl, 80cr, 81cl, 81tr, 81bl, 81br, 82tl, 83bl,
87tc, 91tr, 91bc, 94–95, 98cl;
Crown Copyright. Historic Royal Palaces:
52br, 61cl; **De Beers:** 28tr, 29tr, 31br, 31cla,
52tr, 53cl, 53tl, 53tr, 110br; **Eye Ubiquitous:**
32tl; **Michael Freeman:** 19tl, 30cla, 48–49;
Robert Harding Picture Library: 13br;
Michael Holford: 101tl; **Hulton Getty:** 53br,
111bl; **The Natural History Museum,
London:** 16–17, 16cl, 21crb, 24–25, 26br, 28bc,
30bl, 34tr, 34br, 34bc, 35c, 35cbl, 38cl, 51cr,
104tl; **Rex Features:** 52bl; **Science Photo
Library:** Peter Menzel 30br; David Parker 26tr;
Sotheby's Picture Library: 55tr, 76bl, 85bl;
Smithsonian Institute: 62br, 66cla;
**By Courtesy of the Board of Trustees of the
Victoria and Albert Museum:** 97tr;
The Worshipful Company of Goldsmiths: 79b

Every effort has been made to trace the
copyright holders and we apologise in advance
for any unintentional omissions. We would be
pleased to insert appropriate acknowledgement
in any subsequent edition of this publication.